LOVE, TRUST & Pixie Dust

Leslie G. Green

Love, Trust & Pixie Dust

Second Edition

For information about this title please visit:
www.trustlifetoday.com

Author Photograph by Tracy Allyn Photography

ISBN: 978-0-9899293-0-1

Printed in the United States of America

Dedication

If you have ever asked: *Why me? Why is this happening to me?*, this book is dedicated to you. My wish for you is that somewhere in the pages that follow, the answer becomes clear as it reveals itself to you.

Contents

Introduction

Why Write a Book About Love? About Trust? And What's Pixie Dust?

You will find a lot about love in this book, mostly because love and trust operate much the same. As for pixie dust, be patient on that one....

But this book is mainly about trust. So, why did I write a book about trust? For two reasons:

1. Trust leads directly to what we seek most: Peace.

Although most believe love and happiness are what we seek most, peace is the real show stopper. It is what we seek most, whether we know it or not. Peace is the firm, yet invisible foundation that accompanies love and happiness. Unfortunately, peace is hard to access when you're gripped with fear and worry. It isn't possible to feel a deep sense of peace when you're fearful. The same holds true if you are constantly worried.

This is where trust comes in. After learning to trust, your fear and worry melt away, leaving you wide open and available to experience the peace of a sleeping puppy, content with a warm, full belly of his mother's milk. And once you have peace in your life, strap on your seat belt—love and happiness simply flow!

If peace isn't enough of a reason to write about trust, then what about this?

2. Trust is the backbone of all relationships, from intimate relationships to business relationships to casual relationships. Consider this: Would you continue to see a doctor you didn't trust? Would you put your money in a banking institution you didn't trust? How about allow your children to spend the night at someone's house you didn't trust? Continue to frequent the same coffee shop you didn't trust to get your order right? Trust is that intangible element you can't always put your finger on, but when it's not there, you know it. And fast!

With trust being at the core of any relationship, I find it disturbing I so often hear, "People simply don't trust." People don't trust their government. People don't trust their auto mechanic. People don't trust their lawyers. People don't trust others, period. The bottom line is this: People don't trust themselves. And why should we? Especially considering that when we were children, practically everything we were taught about trust was completely backwards.

If you were taught:

- you must earn trust (from your parents, your teachers, later your bosses...)
- you must prove yourself worthy of trust

- any time you make a mistake, trust can be taken away from you

If you were taught any of these things—and let's be honest, most of us were—you were taught the complete opposite of how trust works. Trust is not external to you. And for that reason, trust cannot be taken away from you. Similarly, you do not need to earn trust. There is no such thing. Stop giving your power away! Trust is not in the hands of the other person. Trust comes from within you *first*.

Once you learn to trust yourself *first*, once you trust yourself to make the right decisions in your life, for your higher good, then you will know the truth about trust. When you experience trust, you are free. Think about that four letter word: F-R-E-E. Free from fear, free from worry, free to live the life of your dreams.

And that's why I've been writing about trust for years on my blog, and now here in this book for you, the person who is ready to learn how to trust.

Within *Love, Trust & Pixie Dust*, you will find stories that illustrate real life examples of trust in action. My sense is that even if you haven't lived the same experiences I have, we're all human; therefore, we are connected because we share certain universal experiences. We have all felt fear and worry. We all seek love and ultimately, peace. And because of that common ground, I hope you find solace and inspiration within the stories, believing that you, too, can learn to trust. And although solace is a good start, my wish for you is that you are able to go beyond and fully understand how to use trust as a tool to benefit you with the big life stuff, the small life stuff, and everything in between.

One last word before we get started: You may be wondering, *why should you trust me?* I mean, you don't know me, I'm a complete stranger. Here's my response: You shouldn't trust me. In fact, don't—not unless my words resonate with you. Only trust what rings true deep inside *you*. Start now by making the shift of placing trust within yourself first. It is my job and honor to serve as your guide while you begin to shift trust inward, by trusting yourself first, trusting others, trusting life.

And please don't ever forget, you are powerful, powerful, powerful.

Love,
Leslie

Prologue

There is a bittersweet feeling in the air. Saying good-bye to a friend moving far away is never easy. Looking at her across the dimly lit kitchen, I get lost in the complex emotion in her eyes, partly hidden by her glasses. Is that a glimmer of happiness I see underneath her mostly somber eyes? Startled back to reality by the ringing of my phone, I see a familiar phone number. But at this time of night? *No, this cannot be good news.* There's enough of a struggle in the atmosphere to keep things light without adding the heaviness of what this phone call will bring.

Seconds later, separated from the party goers, I step into a back room of the house and answer, "Hello, Doctor."

"Leslie? Is that you? Where are you? Sounds like a party."

"Umm, yes." Silence. "A going-away party for a girlfriend. Perhaps this can wait until the morning?"

Audible pause. "Yes, well, I suppose." Another pause. "Yes, I believe it can."

"Thank you, Doctor. Talk to you in the morning."

As I rejoin the party, plastering a smile on my face (more for my own sake), I know my life has just taken a monumental shift. Things will never be the same again.

1

You Are Not Alone

"Surrender isn't giving up. Surrender is going with the currents that are larger than you."
~ Mark Nepo

Meet Trust's Cousin

Within a week of graduating from college, I moved from my native Texas to Mexico City. This first-generation American-born girl, raised by two parents from Mexico, found herself immersed in a culture that felt both reminiscent of her own heartbeat and also that of an alien.

I was surrounded by the same language my parents often spoke to one other, yet with a sing-song cadence that was somehow more. The food was similar to what my mother served at home, but again, somehow more. Mexico City was the land of more. More smells, more traffic, more bustle, more experiences, and more family than I had ever known. And I drank it in.

I spent my first months in Mexico floating about from place to place, meeting cousins for the first time. We are related how? Oh, I see! (Just as quickly forgetting the names of grand-mothers who were sisters.) It didn't matter. I had cousins, and I was moving in with one of them, despite not knowing she even existed a few months prior.

My cousin Roxana and her many dogs (dogs treated more like family members than simple domestic pets—of course we were related!) had an apartment in the heart of a city bigger and more alive than any I had ever known. Shortly after settling in to my cousin's spare bedroom, it was time to find work. I took a job as a speech pathologist, eager to put my freshly earned degree to good use, only to ignore it for the next nineteen years. Now with a little cash flow, I was ready to thoroughly enjoy my new life.

A little less than a year into my stay, a college girlfriend came to visit. Kristi and I snagged the cheapest flight we could find and hopped a plane over to Acapulco, setting out for an ultimate girls' beach weekend. We ate fabulous food, drank fresh coconut juice out of coconuts the size of our heads, and for the most part, enjoyed each other's company by doing what we do best when we're together—laugh!

One morning after breakfast we took a walk on the beach. We were completely engrossed in conversation, so much so, that neither of us noticed the tide and how it had changed. With no glimmer of awareness or hint of what was about to happen, we were both swept up in the undertow. In one large sweep, Kristi was carried far out to sea. She later told me, the harder she swam, the farther out she was pushed. To hear, probably the most optimistic person I know, describe how she was feeling as "hopeless," I knew it must have been bad. She had to have been out there, not only choking on sea water, but also choking with fatigue and fear.

I was experiencing a different battle, although the same hopelessness, fatigue, and fear. I had been caught in the undertow. I remember feeling my body as it was tossed upside down, repeatedly thrown in different directions. I can only imagine I looked similar to my yellow Lab's ragdoll-bear, as she shakes it vigorously, yellow Lab ears flapping side to side, then with the flip of her head, she sends the thing flying into multiple, air-bound cartwheels before landing, limbs splayed this way and that.

I was the ragdoll-bear, unable to stand upright. Every time I tried to right myself, I was forcefully knocked down again. My equilibrium was completely off and soon I didn't know which direction was up or down. The tide had taken me farther down the beach, and the treacherous waves were now slamming me into some nearby rocks. Between the waves, the rocks, and the Acapulco sand (the type filled with coarse, jagged pieces of shell), I felt like hamburger meat that had been pounded until there was no way I could ever be reshaped to my former self.

The Surrender

I'm not sure how long this lasted. I can tell you that the fight I put up was a good one though. I've never fought like that in my life. Ever. Even now as I write about the experience, I can feel my heart begin to race. It was a very intense and disturbing experience. I was completely out of control, using my hands and fingers more as animal-like claws, making every attempt to grip anything I could feel, anything to stabilize myself.

I remember being so tired. Beyond tired. It was in that tired, beat-down state of exhaustion I did something that to this day is the single biggest surprise of my life: *I gave up.* The fight in me was gone, and in the very instant I gave up, I clearly remember saying a prayer of apology. That's right. I didn't pray, "God, please save me." No, I prayed, *"I'm sorry. I give up. I surrender."* As in Nepo's quote, I had chosen to go with a current larger than I.

And as I allowed my muscles to go limp, a man scooped me up. I was being carried like a sack of potatoes, tucked under a stranger's arm, as he ran like hell to get me safely to shore.

At this point, I have to admit something that I've always found extremely interesting about human nature. At least, my human nature. After my brain had processed that the immediate danger had passed, I only had two concerns: 1) where was my friend Kristi? And 2) was my bikini still completely covering my body? (There was a crowd of people encircling me at this point. It seemed a legitimate question.)

Then came a second round of questions: where did this red bikini come from? The one I was wearing was white. And where did the man go? I needed to hug him, to touch his face, to convey gratitude in a way the word *gracias* alone could not do.

I had swallowed a lot of sand and salt water, so it made it very difficult to talk. I was still coming out of fight or flight mode, and my brain wasn't working very well in Spanish, or so I thought. Surely that's why the crowd was looking at me like I was crazy; they just didn't understand me—my Spanish brain must not have kicked in yet. I kept asking about my friend. And where was the man? My friend? The man? There was true urgency, and everyone just kept staring at me. I checked that my bikini was on again (seriously, I was so confused). *Why wasn't anyone doing anything?*

A policeman arrived. Finally, someone who would do something. But no, all he kept asking me was what I had been drinking. According to him, there was no other person involved. There was no friend out at sea and no man. Several bystanders confirmed that there was no man. The police officer began to grab me to help me up, while he continued to question me as to what I had had to drink that morning.

Tiny Speck in the Distance

Now I was fighting-mad. My friend was out there and there had been a man. I have no idea how I did it, but I managed to break loose of the officer's grip, stand up, and push my way through the crowd. I scanned the horizon over and over. At last I saw a tiny speck way out—I mean *way* out—in the distance. And I knew. There was no doubt. That tiny speck in the far off distance was Kristi. I'm not sure how I convinced them to send a boat for her, because I lost consciousness shortly after that. When I woke up, she was sitting next to me. I sneezed and sand flew out of my nose. We looked at each other and began to laugh. My whole body ached. Kristi looked like a drenched rat and I was a bloody mess, with sand flying out of my nose. Laughing seemed like the appropriate reaction at the time.

I haven't told this story many times over the years; it still gives me a great deal of anxiety when I think about it. When I have told it, people tend to focus on the man, thinking he's some kind of unsolved mystery. Did he slip away in all of the commotion? Or maybe I got washed to shore and there really was no man: I was simply delirious. Considering the circumstances, the last option seems plausible. Think what you will. I can tell you exactly what he looked like. He had a big barrel of a stomach, the kind that was hard as a drum. He had shoulder-length, onyx-black hair and kind eyes.

A favorite Bible quote of mine is, *"And when you've done all...stand."* Well, in this story, I tried and I tried to stand, but I literally couldn't. A prayer of surrender, in essence, a prayer to offer "Thy Will Be Done," led me to meet trust's cousin: Surrender. And in that moment I was saved by my very tan, very strong, very fast-running guardian angel.

So when you've done all...stand. Surrender. Trust.

Know that you are not alone. *Believe it.*

A Guiding Force

No matter what language you use: God, Source, Universe, Creator, the Divine—there is a guiding force. We are not left here all alone to wander through life with the hope that all will turn out well. That in some random turn of events, we'll either succeed beyond belief, fail miserably, or something in between. No, we are not alone in our struggles, as we attempt to claw our way to safety, or regain our footing. Nor are we alone in our joys, as we fall in love with Life, with another, with ourselves.

Sometimes, this guiding force comes in the form of an angel. Someone who swoops down in what appears to be a hopeless situation, scoops you up, runs for safety, places your bruised, bloody, and injured body ever so gently on the sand, then disappears.

And sometimes, it's more subtle, more like what we commonly call a coincidence. These coincidences are seen after the fact, after we're able to experience two seemingly unrelated events, yet feel their sameness. Either way, this guiding force is doing just that, guiding us. Where, you might ask? To see Truth. To provide comfort. To bestow the gift of peace. To remind you that you are not alone.

What Language is the Word 'Patience'?

Late one evening I was having a "conversation" with a cousin via text. I had just changed the subject, shifting gears from texting with my cousin-cousin to my doctor-cousin. I was wondering if the aloe vera plant and Vitamin E I had been using on some freakishly large post-surgery scars were what he would recommend to his patients. More to the point, I wanted to know about the Frankenstein factor–When, oh when, will these scars begin to fade?

He responded that yes, aloe vera and Vitamin E are what he would recommend. And as for my Frankenstein comment, he said, "Be patient."

At this point, I should tell you that we had been texting mostly in English, but with some Spanish thrown in for fun every now and then, just to add some spice to our banter.

So after reading his reply of, "Be patient," I texted back, "What language is that, English or Spanish? I don't recognize it."

He responded with, "French. Learn it!"

And so it was that the next day my morning reading, by French entrepreneur turned philosopher/author Jackson Kiddard, was:

"What is PATIENCE?"

Path of least resistance.

Awareness instead of judgment.

Trust what shows up.

Insight instead of assumption.

Empathy for others.

Non-attachment to outcome.

Compassion for yourself.

Easy manifestation of your Highest Potential.

Okay, okay. I get it! The coincidence was not wasted on me. Thank you, Primo. And gracias, Divinity (via Jackson Kiddard), for making sure that I paid attention to my muy inteligente cousin.

This may seem like a silly example of God offering the coincidence of: 1) the last words I read before bedtime urging me to learn the word 'patience', followed by 2) the first thing I read the following morning being entitled, "What is Patience?"

But it wasn't silly to me at the time. Nor is it now. This was one of those more subtle reminders that I am not alone. We are never alone.

~~~~

"We could never learn to be brave and patient, if there were only joy in the world."
~ Helen Keller

(or if there were no large, Frankenstein-like scars to contend with)
~~~~

c-word

I suppose this is as good of a time as any to introduce the c-word (lowercase 'c' please, I don't like to give it too much power or energy).

The doctor from the Prologue, the one who called my mobile phone during my friend's going-away party, was a radiologist. She was calling to deliver a diagnosis of breast cancer.

cancer is tough to introduce into any conversation for the first time; at least that's been my experience. Once said out loud, it's out there. Real.

Though not a focus of this book, my experience with breast cancer provided enormous opportunities to practice deep trust on the inside as well as focus on my emotional state. I was also challenged and stretched in ways I could not have imagined, as the call to practice patience with the outside of my body appeared at every turn. As I regained physical strength. As I learned to humble myself and ask for help. As the large scars, so clearly visible as the undisguised reminders that they were (still are), slowly fade away.

On August 4, 2011, this is what I shared with my readers on my blog as I introduced the topic:

"See Me as Whole, Leslie's Healing"

Sitting...sitting...sitting. Writing, backspace, delete. More writing, more backspace, delete. Twenty minutes later...still sitting. I know exactly what I want to write, but for once, I have no idea how to start. Okay, dive in.

A little over two weeks ago I was diagnosed with breast cancer. I found no lump. I was simply going in for my first mammogram at age forty. That's right: no lump, first mammogram.

I decided to start today's post with the facts, urging those of you who have put off having a mammogram because you haven't felt anything through your monthly self-examination, to please reconsider. As I said, I felt no lump, because there was no lump. There are different types of breast cancer, and the type I have [had] is located within the ductal system and cannot be felt through self-examination. It's commonly called DCIS (ductal carcinoma in situ), of which there are different grades and subtypes. Without getting into too much detail, my subtype is called Micropapillary DCIS, which makes the flashing red light in my breast surgeon's brain go off. She described it as "the bad-acting DCIS and therefore must be treated promptly and aggressively."

One of the many pieces of good news is that it was caught early! And how fortunate, in this day and age, that within these two-plus weeks, I have been able to meet with a multitude of surgeons, complete more tests and evaluations than I'd care to recap, and still manage to take an abbreviated family vacation and steal away for a short girl's weekend of "me time."

As you see, life goes on, as it should, and must. This is merely a blip, as my friend so eloquently put it, *"Your natural state is perfection and this is a small blip on your way back to perfection."* (Thank you, Anne.)

This I can assure you: I am not worried. Apprehensive, yes: This is a new experience for me. But worried? No. I am precisely where I'm supposed to be, and I've hand-picked the precise surgeons to form part of my Healing Team. This team came together in a unique and organic way to support me and ensure my physical and emotional health. But the blessings began well before the medical team was in place.

Meet FAITH and Faith

A few years ago I met an extraordinary group of women. They each held a common desire to study FAITH *(Finding Authenticity, Integrity, Truth, and Harmony)*. Through their collective love and spirit, as well as the love and support from my family and dear friends, I felt I was already ahead of the curve when my radiologist delivered the news to me. All of the studying I've done throughout the years on trust, on various spiritual matters, on knowing the Divine—it has all prepared me for today, a place where I stand strong and confident in spirit, yet wise enough (finally) to know that it's okay to be vulnerable, too.

So it was only fitting when I stopped by my radiologist's office to pick up my mammogram films that the doctor took me aside, and as we embraced, she placed a stuffed animal named Faith in my arms.

This Faith is also an acronym, although not written in all caps. Her name stands for *Friends Always In The Heart*. She came about by one of my radiologist's patients years ago. To this day, my doctor lovingly hands out Faith-the-Lamb to all of her newly diagnosed patients, along with a little piece of her heart as she speaks candidly with you.

Attached to Faith's ear was a tag (which I now keep in my wallet). It says:

> "Cancer is so limited,
> It cannot cripple love.
> It cannot shatter hope.
> It cannot corrode faith.
> It cannot destroy peace.
> It cannot kill friendship.
> It cannot suppress memories.
> It cannot silence courage.
> It cannot invade the soul.
> It cannot steal eternal life.
> It cannot conquer the spirit."
> ~ Anonymous

It's as if the events of my life have sandwiched me between FAITH and Faith. What an incredibly blessed woman I am.

As I honor that blessing, I have chosen to share with you, through my writing, as many lessons as are appropriate. Other than here on my blog, I will not be accepting phone calls or responding to emails on this topic—I commit to only breathe positivity into this healing experience. And although answering questions may appear to be a neutral act, my experience has been that it's extremely draining for me.

I want each one of you to know how grateful I am, knowing many of you will be sending me prayers, love, light, and healing energy. For that, *Thank You.*

During these next months, as I live and breathe true trust, I ask one thing of you, and one thing only. That you: *See Me as Whole, as Healed.*

In the present tense, I ask that you see me as whole and healed now. As if it is already done.

And so it is.

Love,
Leslie

~~~~

Now think of yourself, think of a time you've been faced with a new experience that could fall into the category of fearful or the unknown. Maybe it was a diagnosis, or it could have been any major life-changing event. Isn't it comforting to know that you were not alone? I am reminded of this every time I get in my car and look down in the drink holder, where the following quote has winked up at me for over three years: *"God dwells within me...as me."*

God dwells within you, as you. God dwells within each one of us.
~~~~

Swooshed Away, The Faith of a Child

Despite knowing that God dwells within us, sometimes it takes the faith and the innocence of a child to remind our grown-up selves to see the God within, as we pray, believe, let go, and ultimately, trust.

A few years ago, exactly three days before school let out for Christmas break, I received a call from school. On the other end of the line, there was sobbing. No words, just sobbing. The sound can only be described as raw and gut-wrenching. It took me several moments to determine 1) exactly which son was responsible for such a noise and 2) that neither of them was hurt or in danger. Only then was I able to listen and begin to process what in the world had happened to create such a reaction.

As my then third-grader was on his way home from school that afternoon, he was barely managing to clench a piece of artwork and its three contest ribbons to the handlebars of his scooter. The piece of artwork was large enough to be cumbersome and the ribbons delicate enough to be a nuisance *without* having to manage a scooter on a terribly windy day. Add all that together and *voila*: you have a total recipe for disaster.

When my son finally found his voice, he explained that the wind came "swooshing in." He had managed to keep his grip on the artwork, but lost the ribbons that were paper-clipped to it. "My ribbons! My contest ribbons are gone!" More sobs, as he relived the experience in the story-telling of it.

He was heartbroken. Devastated might be more accurate. As soon as I hung up the phone, I grabbed the dog, jumped in the car, and arrived at the trails behind his school within minutes.

Since he saw the ribbons swoosh away, we knew they hadn't fallen off inside the school. That left the bike trail or possibly the creek below. We combed every possible inch for his three missing ribbons, backtracking several times to double and triple check; the wind was not letting up a bit. I knew at any second we would spot the red, yellow, and rainbow-colored ribbons he had described.

Long story short, we looked and looked and found *n-o-t-h-i-n-g* that resembled ribbons.

Spontaneous Prayer

Defeat set in. The tears came back, slow and quiet this time. Shoulders slumped, he turned back and we headed for the car. It was apparent that we had done all we could do. In that moment, I again remembered that favorite quote: *And when you've done all...stand.* So I reminded him to have faith. Stand. He paused and looked up at me, asking if this was a good time to "trust life?" As I nodded, he said a quick prayer out loud.

Filled with emotion brought on by his spontaneous prayer, I felt moved to talk to him more about trusting life—to remind him now that he had prayed, it was time to *let go*. Time to let go of the worry and to trust the ribbons would find him. I reminded him that the ribbons could come back to him in many different ways. They might blow past him tomorrow on his way to school, or maybe he would find them at recess later that week. "It doesn't matter how they make their way back to you," I explained. "That's not your concern. What matters is that you believe they will. You *believe* they will find you."

Just In Case

The next morning, I called the school and explained to one of the school secretaries what had happened. I asked if it was possible to replace the ribbons (just in case). She said she really didn't think so—the art competition was district wide, and because it wasn't done at the school level, replacing the ribbons would be difficult. I went ahead and emailed the art teacher to see if there was anything she could do (just in case). No luck. She wouldn't be back until school resumed in January.

After I had done everything I could think to do as a mother, I again heard the voice in my head, *And when you've done all...stand.* So I stood. And I waited. And my son waited.

By Friday, I was hoping my son was starting to forget about the ribbons, the prayer, trusting, all of it. When during my morning workout, the phone rang. On the other end of the line was Cathy, the same secretary I had spoken to earlier in the week about the swooshed ribbons.

She said, "Leslie, you're never going to believe this! Let me read you this note I found on my desk this morning." She read:

> "Good Morning Dee,
> Mae found these ribbons outside of school—before they blew away. Don't know if there is a way to get them back to the person who earned them?
> See you tomorrow!
> Jacqueline C."
>
> (She couldn't make out the last name.)

By the way, I never found out who Dee, Mae, or Jacqueline were. Angels?

To Believe, To Trust

My smile broadened with every word Cathy read. Who would have thought? How did the note end up on Cathy's desk—the same secretary I spoke to about the ribbons? Why not one of the other two secretaries who wouldn't have had a clue and who may have just tossed them in the trash? And remarkable also, this happened on the Friday before Christmas break, one of Cathy's busiest days of the year as she checks in tons of parents for holiday parties. Why didn't the whole thing just fall through the cracks somehow?

Because my son believed. Because he trusted. He trusted in prayer, in life, in something bigger than he. He trusted that it was being taken care of. And he knew he didn't have to be the one to figure out *how* his ribbons would get back to him—all he had to do was *let go and believe, trusting life* would take care of the rest. (At this point, you might be asking, *What's the difference between trust and faith?* The simple definition of trust is to follow your heart. We use faith in a higher power in order to trust ourselves.)

How fortunate I am to be surrounded by teachers of trust. Teachers of Life. Even if this teacher was only eight years old at the time.

How do you trust? With the faith of a child? Or was your childhood such that faith and trust were foreign concepts, so foreign you find it difficult to trust now that you are an adult? If the latter is you, remember, you are not alone.

~~~~~

"I had to trust life, since I was young enough to believe that life loved the person who dared to live it."
~ Maya Angelou
~~~~~

2

Fear Vs. Love Vs. Trust

"Purpose, energy, power to do,
and all strong thoughts cease
when doubt and fear creep in."
~ from As A Man Thinketh, by
James Allen

Common Denominator of Fear

It's often said that trust is the glue that holds our world together. As small children, we learn to walk, talk, and interact with others and our surroundings within the framework of trust. Trust is the foundation on which we build our lives. By using our five senses, we begin to trust life and how it works. A certain smell means food is on its way, a bell sounding announces there is someone at the door, a loud whistle means Mother's water is ready for tea. You scoot too closely to Mom as she sips delicately from her cup and you hear, "Careful...hot." Little by little you add to your ever-growing foundation. Imagine how terrifying life would be without a foundation of trust, how utterly unpredictable your life would feel if you didn't trust the ground would remain beneath you when you took your next step.

Eventually though, fears creep in. Maybe you are bitten by a spider you innocently come upon with curiosity. Or you inhale pool water while learning to swim and the burning sensation forms an unpleasant memory. Or you wander off from your family in a crowded mall, temporarily lost and alone.

Many years later, having reached adulthood, what are you afraid of now? Spiders still? Public speaking? Failure? Death? Those four typically hit the top 10 lists of common fears. When it comes to spiders, there are many who love these little eight-legged creatures, and in fact, have chosen to dedicate their lives studying them. Public speaking? There are those, myself included, who relish being on a stage; the feeling when a connection is made with the audience feels like pure, positive electricity coursing through my veins.

While I don't know anyone who is chomping at the bit to fail, there are many lessons to be learned from failure. Thomas Edison, when asked about his numerous attempts to patent the light bulb, allegedly said, "I have not failed. I've just found 10,000 ways that won't work."

And as for death? Yes, naturally there are those who fear it. However, others in extreme pain and suffering may welcome it, perhaps even long for it. And yet there are others who would agree with Lao Tzu, who said, "Life and death are one thread, the same line viewed from different sides."

All this speculating about fear brings us back to the original question: *What are you really afraid of?* What do these fears, plus hundreds more, share as a common denominator? *The unknown.*

Spiders: *"I better not get too close. What if it bites me? That will hurt! I may even have to go to the hospital." Enter, the unknown.*

Public speaking: *"I could get up there and forget everything. Worse yet, I could be brilliant and no one gets it, their eyes glaze over and the grocery lists in their minds start to form." Again, the unknown.*

Failure: *"If I try my absolute hardest and put all my heart and effort into this undertaking only to fail in the end, why bother?" The unknown.*

Death: *"It's so finite, permanent. Or is it? What happens? I just don't know. How can I know for sure?" Yet again, the unknown.*

Consider this....

Knowing When You Are Predicted to Die

One day, while listening to satellite radio, I heard about the controversy around a future over-the-counter blood test that claims it will be able to predict your life expectancy. I'm a closet anatomy nerd, someone who reads medical studies and reports "for fun," so I'll try not to get too geeky on the anatomy/physiology side of things.

First, there are these things called telomeres that are located on the tips of our chromosomes. Scientists believe that the shorter they are, the closer we are to dying. Currently there are tests that predict lifespan based on lifestyle and medical conditions and history, but this is the first test that uses blood to estimate life expectancy. A simple, straight forward, and, yes, over-the-counter test to predict how long you'll live.

A few hours after listening to the radio program, I was sorting through stacks of old notebooks in my office. I opened one of the notebooks and began flipping through its pages, landing on a particular entry about three years old. At the top of the page, the header read, *"If I knew I had a fatal disease, would I live my life differently?"* Hmm.... How interesting the way life presents information, or perhaps more accurately, *messages*, for us.

Dated 9/21/08, nearly three years prior to the radio show I was listening to (May of 2011). In my own handwriting, the note reads:

> If I knew I had a fatal disease, would I live my life differently?
>
> Yes.
>
> How?
>
> - tons more patience with everyone...with LIFE; no need for anger
> - face fears head-on, not push fears in the back of my head, not make them bigger and allow my mind to invent fiction that spins out of control
> - be Real with others, all the time
> - look for love in all situations, not fear"

The first thing that struck me, of course, was the synchronicity of the news piece I had heard earlier in the day and the content of the page I was staring at. They mirrored each other. Next, was the language I used. Three years ago, as I scribbled in a notebook, I used much of the same language, and in the same way as I do today in my blog: Real with a capital R, writing about fear versus love, LIFE, often in all caps.

What was this serendipitous moment here to teach me? Life was urging me to hit the pause button, ponder the question, absorb the response. Okay. So I paused, pondered, and absorbed. And what I came up with was a bigger question:

Why would it take believing I had a fatal disease in order for me to live by those few bullet points above? I mean, there's nothing terribly WOW about anything I jotted down. I didn't say, "I'll travel around the world, blowing all the money known to man!" What I listed were simple, basic things. Simple things that made me wonder how close had I come, three years later, to living that list? How close are you today to living your list?

What feelings surface for you when I ask, "How well do you trust the unknown?"

Falling Into the Unknown

A group of frogs set off on a long hike, traveling through the woods. Two of the frogs fell into a deep pit. When their companions saw how deep the pit was, they told the two frogs not to bother jumping—they were as good as dead! The two frogs ignored the comments and began to jump with all their might, determined that their next jump would be the one to launch them up and out of the pit of despair.

But the other frogs just kept shouting at them to stop, repeating that the two were as good as dead. Finally, one of the frogs lost heart and gave into fear. He believed what the other frogs were saying and stopped jumping.

He fell down and died.

The other frog continued to jump as hard as he could. Once again, the crowd of frogs yelled at him to stop his pain and just die. He jumped even harder and finally made it out.

When he got out, the other frogs said, "Didn't you hear us?"

The frog explained that he was deaf. He thought they were encouraging him the entire time!

Lessons For the *Giver* of Words:

- There is power of life and death in the tongue. An encouraging word to someone who is down can lift them up and help them make it through the day.
- A destructive word to someone who is down or fearful can be all it takes to destroy them.

Lessons For the *Receiver* of Words:

- Be careful what you choose to believe.
- Be mindful of who you choose to follow.
- And whether you hear as well as a cat burglar, ready to flee the scene of the crime at the slightest noise, or as poorly as an artist-in-flow, creating a Divine masterpiece, take heed to what serves you and your purpose. Hear that, trust that. Be the artist-in-flow, tune out all the rest.

Speak Life and Love to those who cross your path. Anyone can speak words that rob another of the spirit to continue in difficult times. Special is the person who takes the time to encourage another.

Knowing Too Much

We can likely all agree that to some extent, the unknown feels scary. But, how about the opposite? How about knowing too much? Can that also feel scary?

While on our way to a doctor's appointment, my son and I drove quietly, listening to music. He and I spend a lot of time together in the car, usually full of chatter, but this day was different, he was very quiet. Was he simply enjoying the music? Was he thinking? As we sat at a traffic light, I glanced over at him. Furrowed brow, eyes narrowed. He was definitely thinking. It was the type of thinking a mother does not interrupt.

As we pulled into the parking lot, my son's quiet, contemplative spell was beginning to lift. As I removed the key from the ignition, he looked over at me and said, "Sometimes getting older scares me because I know too much."

"I know what you mean," I replied, nodding slowly. There was nothing left to say.

What I believe my son was actually referring to was *becoming aware*—the opposite of "Ignorance is bliss." In a flash, you go from not knowing any better, to knowing in such a way that Life has taught you lessons that cannot be untaught—or for that matter, unlearned. And to a child, I imagine that the knowledge of this new responsibility might feel scary. The more we understand about Life, the more accountable we must hold ourselves to being true to who we are. (More accountable can sometimes feel scary.) And in today's culture, that's not always the easiest or most popular thing to do. But it's the task one is faced with, once *aware*.

So, is the topic here knowing too much? Or is knowing too much simply a product of becoming aware? Once aware, you no longer believe you are alone. You regain your faith and begin to trust in Life, in a higher force. Remember the difference between trust and faith? To trust is to follow your heart. We use faith in a higher power in order to trust ourselves.

From the unknown to knowing too much. Either way, *A Course in Miracles,* written by Helen Schucman, says, "If you knew Who walks beside you on this way which you have chosen, fear would be impossible." Which I translate to say, "If you knew Who truly walks beside you, how could you choose anything other than trust?"

A Course in Miracles also tells us that every human act has at its base either love or fear. We approach situations, react to others, and are motivated by one of these two positions. Another way to think of it is that all acts are either an act of love or a cry for love (fear). Either way, the only appropriate response is to give love.

Shining a Light on Fear

"There are two basic motivating forces: fear and love. When we are afraid, we pull back from life. When we are in love, we open to all that life has to offer with passion, excitement, and acceptance. We need to learn to love ourselves first, in all our glory and our imperfections. If we cannot love ourselves, we cannot fully open to our ability to love others or our potential to create. Evolution and all hopes for a better world rest in the fearlessness and open-hearted vision of people who embrace life."

~ John Lennon

~~~~

I was talking to a girlfriend late one night on the phone. As Lisa and I were talking, I remembered an article I had read by Martha Beck, I think it was, in which she discussed how our motivations are driven by either fear or love. I no longer have the article, but I did jot down a few notes which I kept. Here is what I captured:
~~~~

FEAR	LOVE
Always feels bad	Always feels good
Motivates grasping	Motivates liberation
Seizes control	Relaxes control
Insists on certainty	Accepts uncertainty
Needs everything	Needs nothing

Nice list, right? But here's the thing: if you're anything like I am, my mind can tend to play a fine game of "sit and spin" on the fear side. And when I'm actively participating on the fear side, there's always some well-meaning person there to remind me, "If you would *just* change your thinking...." To which, I typically respond with one of two things:

1. "That's easier said than done." I use this response when I'm not ready to change, still very much clinging to the fear side. This is when my ego-mind has gripped my higher self and I am looking through my hopeless-tinted glasses.

Or, I respond with

2. "How?" and a slight tilt of the head. This is when I truly want to take action and make a change. I'm tired of my old way. I'm ready to see that it has not been serving me well and I'm finally aware of that fact. Along with this newfound awareness comes the willingness and desire to change.

You have to want to change in order to make change. Change can be easy once we genuinely want it.

But *how?*

The how lies in *love.*

Flipping Fear

Much of what we experience that feels "bad" is really what we've created for ourselves that has a foundation in fear. But, what if we were able to flip it? What if we were able to make a shift? When I flip it and concentrate on the love side in the list above, I can walk through almost any situation and my experience changes. It's almost like magic!

The key is to catch yourself during the spinning and acknowledge what's happening, to become aware. (Over years of self-observation, I've identified that my breathing gives me away every time. Breathe from my chest = anxiety, which is fear based. Breathe from my abdomen = a state of peace, which is love based.)

After I identify what's happening, I usually let out a sigh of relief. My ego can no longer play a game of mental gymnastics with me. How do you determine when you're approaching a situation from fear or from love? Are you also able to use how you're breathing as a clue? Or do you have a different method you use?

That is to say, the next time you find yourself in a situation that feels "bad," or you feel as if you're grasping, or trying to seize control, let your gut be your guide over to the love side. As you walk into love, pay attention to what it is you're trying to control and ask yourself:

- Does this feel good? Do I feel good?
- Does this feel free? Do I feel free?
- Have I relaxed my feelings of control over this situation?
- Have I released any expectations over the outcome?

Boil it down there. And if you still have discomfort, realize where it lies within the questions and investigate the fear further until it gives way. Pinpointing where the fear remains is a powerful liberator. Once you see where your fear is trying to hide, you can shine the light on it until you feel love begin to take root. Continue to shine the light, stay with it, and gradually feel the love settle within your heart.

After all, isn't that what we all desire? To feel love, not fear? To trust, not fear? Love and trust are very similar in that regard, and in many, many more ways as well.

Strategy for Overcoming Fear

I have a good friend I used to work with who would speak of her "little red wagon" and all of the tools she carried around inside it. Each time she learned a new skill, she'd toss it over her shoulder, having it land squarely in her little red wagon, ready for easy access when she needed it. Sometimes we would be brainstorming a project at work and I'd share something with her that she would especially like. I could always tell because her eyes would light up...and in that moment, I knew she was throwing my advice, suggestion, or technique into her wagon. To this day, when I learn a new skill that I'm particularly fond of, I visualize myself throwing it into my own little red wagon.

Several months ago, a different friend, Heather, asked me to write an article on being positive. I thought at the time, There are sooooo many articles out there already on the subject of being positive. What angle do I have that's fresh or different? I couldn't come up with a single thing, so I promptly dismissed the request. Later, Heather mentioned it again to me, so I started giving it some serious thought. The thing is, I have not been sure where to start. Not until I remembered that I have my own little red wagon, and as my mind rummaged through it to find where my positivity comes from, I realized it just IS. Hmm, well, how is that going to help my friend? Okay, Heather, just BE positive! There you go! How's that working for you? No, no, no. That won't do. So I dug a little deeper, and I realized much of my positive attitude is based on overcoming fears. And that, I do have a strategy for! That, I can write about. It's a strategy I have used basically my entire life: visualization. As it turns out, while I was trying to visualize all of the tools in my wagon, it became apparent that visualization is one of my tools.

Cultivating a Practice to Overcome Fears

When I was six years old, we lived out in the country and kept cattle. If I wanted to go anywhere fun, I knew it meant jumping on my bike, but it also meant crossing our cattle guard. Now, for those of you who can't picture a cattle guard, there are different types, but in general they are made out of long metal cylinders placed side by side, several inches apart, making it impossible for cows to cross and extremely bumpy for anything with tires. (For example, my peach-colored Huffy bike with those squishy handlebars I remember my sweaty, little hands loved squeezing).

At first my brothers demonstrated how to cross on their bikes, which of course looked easy. But I, being this person who lives in her head, could only imagine the bike jerking my arms, the front tire turning, the Huffy bike coming to a halt, and little Leslie being thrown off onto the hard, uneven surface below. The more I pictured that scene, the more real it became. And the more my mind made me my own prisoner—on my side of the cattle guard, not on the other side where friends, the pool, hamburgers, french fries doused in a bucket of ketchup, and a jukebox playing bad 70s music awaited me.

I remember thinking I had to change my thoughts before the "bad" ones stuck. So I did. I started to visualize myself, not only crossing the cattle guard, but also feeling all of the bumps, which I imagined as feeling exhilarating, not scary. Most importantly, however, was feeling myself *already* safely on the other side. For me, I needed to picture the positive outcome, believe it, and *feel* it. *It felt like freedom!* And that's all it took. I crossed that day. And crossed back to return home later that afternoon, using the same technique. And the next day, and the next. I remember using that technique longer than I'd like to admit before it became "easy."

Using my visualization technique with something as concrete as crossing a cattle guard has served me well in the many years that have followed since I was six years old. I've also been able to use it on intangible things as well. I visualize positive outcomes often. I believe they *already are* while conjuring the feelings I'll have—whether they be love, freedom, or simply to be seen and heard for who I truly am.

Try it for yourself. The more you use the visualization technique, the easier it gets. And by the way, I'm not talking about the Law of Attraction here, visualization is different. Again and again I've witnessed people become bitter or cynical, sometimes even declare they are a failure when what they've focused on attracting never comes to pass. That is so far from the truth. The truth is, we are all magnificent beings. So, instead of attracting, think *allowing*. Visualizing and allowing go hand-in-hand.

Visualize your desired outcome. Allow it, with no expectations. Then completely let go, leading to trust. See, at the core of trusting, is letting go. Letting go is so vital to trusting, to Life really, an entire chapter is dedicated to it. I believe in letting go, but I also know firsthand that letting go can be difficult. Our minds latch onto images of crashing our bikes and all sorts of other fictions that haven't happened, robbing us of positive experiences. But if it's positivity you're looking for in your life, take a peek in your wagon and see what is in there. You might be surprised. And if you don't like what you see, or if you're stuck and think your wagon looks kind of bare, pay particular attention to the stories in this book and others that people share with you. Toss in the stories that speak to you—that guide you on your journey—toss them directly in your wagon. Keep them close for easy access.

Thank you, Suzanne, for showing me how to use my wagon. And thank you, Heather, for not letting me off the hook, for having me dig around in my wagon long enough to find the buried treasure.

There Are Game-Changers, and There Are Life-Changers

There are so many stories in life! Think about it, we have:

- bedtime stories (I still tell these to one very imaginative eleven-year-old who will not let his beloved Hedgie-Stories be put to rest.)
- love stories
- family stories
- ghost stories
- fairytales
- fables
- fishing stories (I tell ya, it was *this* big!)
- pregnancy or labor and delivery stories (every parent has at least one of these—per child!)
- and then there are the stories we tell ourselves (true, or not-so-true)

In my forty-three years, I imagine I've either told or been told *thousands* of stories! Hundreds of thousands. Out of those stories, I have my favorites like we all do. There are favorites to be cherished, and there are game-changers, and then there are life-changers.

I'd like to share a Life-Changer with you:

"A Warrior and His Bride"

There is a famous Sufi story:

> A man just got married and was returning home with his wife. They were crossing a lake in a boat when suddenly a great storm arose.
>
> Although the husband was a strong warrior and had always protected her, the wife became very much afraid because it seemed hopeless. The boat was small, but the storm was huge, and at any moment they were going to be drowned. But the man sat silently, calm and quiet, as if nothing were happening.
>
> The woman was trembling and she said, "Are you not afraid? This may be our last moment of life! It doesn't seem that we will be able to reach the shore. Only some miracle can save us; otherwise, death is certain. Are you not afraid? Are you mad? Are you a stone or something?"
>
> The man laughed and took his sword out of its sheath. The woman was even more puzzled. What was he doing? Then he brought the sword close to the woman's neck—so close that just a small gap was present. It was almost touching her neck. He said, "Are you afraid?"

She started to laugh and said, "Why should I be afraid? If the sword is in your hands, why should I be afraid? I know you love me."

He put the sword away and said, "This is my answer. I know the power I call God. He loves me, and the sword is in His hands, as the storm is in His hands—so whatever is going to happen is going to be good. If we survive, good; if we don't survive, good. No matter what happens, Thy Will Be Done."

~~~~

This is the trust one must imbibe. Such tremendous trust is capable of transforming your whole life. And *only* such tremendous trust is capable of transforming your life. Less than that will not do.

This story illustrates many things: fear for one's life, the questioning of a loved one's sanity, deep trust. The trust we either have in the Divine or we don't. The trust we either have in Life or we don't. And if we *do* have that trust deeply anchored within us, what reason is there to fear?

This story was handed to me on a piece of paper by a dear friend; he thought it coupled nicely with the messages I had been sharing through my writing. But here's the backstory: The previous year, our older son had been diagnosed with a rare kidney disease. Since that
~~~~

time, I had been doing my best to learn about the condition, getting him settled into his new hearing aids (this condition affects ears, eyes, and kidneys), and introducing him to a slew of new doctors. My husband and I also spent time understanding what impacts on our son's life we should prepare for based on this diagnosis. I then began implementing necessary changes to his routine such as altering his diet, beginning monthly acupuncture sessions, and keeping a nightly acupressure regimen.

These were necessary steps to provide the best health and overall living conditions for my son. They were also steps I could control. Providing a kidney-friendly diet, scheduling and making sure he arrived to his doctor's appointments, administering both Eastern and Western medicine, ensuring he gets adequate rest—these were all things I could control to the extent that a mother can. Beyond that, I came to the slow and sobering realization that I could not control much else. I could not control my son's fate. I could not control whether he suffers physically or emotionally due to this condition, any more than I could control when it would manifest fully. To experience pain myself is one thing, but my child? How do I sleep at night knowing that one day he will be faced with more than any child should have to endure? When do my husband and I tell him about this diagnosis, so we're able to strike the balance of allowing him to retain as much of his childhood innocence and freedom as possible, free of unnecessary worries, fears, and burdens while still preparing him for what's to come? What does all of this, and much more, look like? There's so much I cannot control. So much that lies in the realm of the unknown.

Approximately a year following my son's diagnosis, after preparing the changes to his diet, after introducing him to his new doctors, and having him settled into his new routines, I began to notice an unfamiliar feeling. It was a feeling of dis-ease within me that had nestled its way into my cells; I could feel it right below the surface of my skin. That is when the Sufi story I just shared with you was given to me. As I sat in my friend's office reading the story of the warrior and his bride, the sneeze from a butterfly could have knocked me over as the dis-ease I had been storing was steadily replaced by the significance in a key Truth that appears in the last line. As subtle as a whisper, you may gloss over it if you're not paying attention: the warrior said to his bride, "If we survive, good; if we don't survive, good—no matter what happens, *Thy Will Be Done.*"

No matter what happens, Thy Will Be Done. No matter what happens during my son's journey, I accept. Thy Will Be Done. I surrender. Thy Will Be Done. Trusting, trusting, knowing, believing, Thy Will Be Done.

Amen.

~~~~

"Happy* is the mother who can say sincerely, that she puts her child in God's hands, and knows therefore, that he is divinely protected."

~ Florence Scovel Shinn

(*Happy? Hmm.... Maybe not *happy*, more like peaceful. I'll take peace over this situation any day. And so it is.)
~~~~

3

It Is What It Is

"My life has been filled with many misfortunes, most of which never happened."

~ Mark Twain

Why Should You Trust Life?

Clichés become clichés mostly because they speak the truth. So whether you loathe or love the cliché *It Is What It Is*, there's a whole lot of truth in it. That said, why should we even bother trusting?

One of my dear friends decided to play Devil's Advocate one day, and sent me an email asking, "*Why* should we trust life?" I say Devil's Advocate because he wasn't asking the question expecting a response, but rather for me to consider how I'd respond to someone reading my blog or even to you sitting here now, holding this book and wondering, *Yeah, why should I trust life?*

There is a simple, one-word response to the question—and that word is: *Peace*. Being at peace in our everyday lives is the ultimate end goal and reason behind why we trust. Trust unlocks the door to peace. But there's more....

The Crux of the Matter: What IS versus What IF

Peace is why we trust, yes, but there's more. First off, put yourself in the mindset of thinking of trusting life as a series of events. The series starts with the awareness/acceptance of What IS, which in many cases is the same as letting go.

Essentially, What IS, is looking at a situation and NOT inserting layer upon layer of What IF: "What IF I lose my job? What IF he leaves me? What IF I get sick?" No, no, no. What IS means being grounded in seeing the truth, in not inventing the stuff that makes our heads spin out of control.

Think: whatever you are worrying about or holding on to (the *What IF*) and imagine yourself letting go of those *What IFs* and seeing *What Truly IS.*

Once you are aware and accept *What IS*, the enormous amount of energy you were giving to the worry—or the *What IFs*—now ends. It has no power over you. This is key, because before you are aware and accept *What IS*, your mind races with thoughts of worry and fear. Thoughts of *What IF* often lead to the invention of entirely fictitious situations (which I, and Mark Twain might add, hardly ever end up happening). These ungrounded thoughts are what take up so much unnecessary energy. They often lead to more worry, more fear. You become restless and irritable, you lose sleep. The snowball effect is in full force at this point. The "monkey-mind" is cranked up in high gear, jumping from one thought to another and another, not easily quieted. I think it's pretty safe to say we've all experienced monkey-mind to one degree or another.

Field of Pure Awareness

It is when we become aware, and accept *What IS*, that the monkey-mind quiets, and we can Be. Once we are in a state of Being, we are able to observe moment by moment, from the highest field of all, Pure Awareness.

Now, if it has all made sense up to this point, but I just lost you with the Pure Awareness comment, hang tight. I want to take it a step further and deeper. Once you're observing moment by moment, no longer in the worry-place and completely out of the monkey-mind chatter, whatever action you take will be in harmony with this field of Pure Awareness. Therefore, whatever action you take will be for the highest good for all. (Remember the Sufi story of the warrior and his bride?)

By trusting life, we accept *What IS*, quieting the conflict in the monkey-mind and freeing us to observe and then act from Pure Awareness, which will be for the highest good of all. Operating for the highest good of all also takes us to the next level: Life is not just about us at an individual level, but as living beings we are all connected in a very intimate way. For that reason, operating for the highest good of all is something to strive for.

By trusting, we marry our free will with the Divine, knowing that we are taken care of. We are not alone in our worries or our struggles. We are never alone.

You are never alone.

I have attempted to explain in words what is a *knowing* within me. I encourage you to add to these concepts, question them, mold them and make them yours, changing the verbiage to suit your taste. In doing so, you will land on your Truth, something that resonates and works for you.

Take a moment to consider how you typically approach life. Which side of the cattle guard do you tend to hang out on? The *What IF* side or the *What IS* side? Where you are on the spectrum will immediately tell you what your beliefs are about how trust works. And by the way, this has nothing to do with religion. You may be the most religious person out there, attending every mass and service offered, yet between each mass, each service—maybe even during each one—you're worrying about all of the *What IFs* in your life. Becoming aware and accepting *What IS* is a spiritual belief and practice that anyone can adopt, regardless of religious beliefs.

Chinese Symbol for Crisis

Three Stories of "*What IS*"

Friend 1

As you know, at age forty I scheduled my first, and last, mammogram. A week before I went into the hospital for a bilateral mastectomy, I was talking to a dear friend on the phone. She had wholeheartedly embraced my request of seeing me as Whole and Healed in the present tense. She told me she had no other way of seeing me. She said there was this tugging in the back of her mind that said, "It isn't even real. The surgeons are going to get in there next week and say, 'Oops, Leslie. Looks like we made a mistake! There actually is no cancer.' That's how Whole and Healed I see you." (Thank you, Amy.)

Friend 2

A different girlfriend called later that afternoon; evidently she had heard "the news." She began by saying how sorry she was about my *crisis*. I was confused, or perhaps just a little slow. I wasn't sure to what she was referring. My first thought was of the bad weather that had hit the East Coast and all the friends I had there. Perhaps there had been some new development I hadn't heard of relating to Hurricane Irene.

However, as she continued talking, I quickly understood that she was talking about *me.*

Two different people. Two different perceptions that lay on opposite ends. One based in love. The other based in fear.

For the record, I wasn't upset by the second friend who called—I understand that we all process and deal with these sorts of things very differently. I only offer it up to show the contrast between the two. It's a contrast that led me to think about one of the rotating quotes on the bottom of my email signature. It reads:

"The Chinese symbol for 'crisis' combines figures that depict both danger and opportunity."

Danger and opportunity. What a thought-provoking, curious, and accurate depiction of the word *crisis.*

Friend 3, Pulling Up Anchor

Keep in mind the timeline of when this story was taking place—this was *after* the diagnosis, but *before* I underwent the bilateral mastectomy. For Friend 1, *What IS* spoke to her with, "Leslie, you are already Whole, already Healed." For Friend 2, *What IS* was a crisis. Enter Friend 3....

As I walked into my friend's office, he launched right into, "So, who are your doctors?

Are you comfortable with who you've chosen? When is the surgery scheduled?" Then he paused, and said, "I'm sorry to be so matter-of-fact...I don't mean to diminish what you're going through by jumping right into the core of it, but I figure you've already pulled up anchor. I don't want to keep you back *there*," gesturing with his hands, "when you're way over *here*."

What an incredible gift my friend shared with me: *The gift of meeting someone where they are*. It's a skill my buddy Matt modeled beautifully, and one I'd like to emulate. I see it as a skill high on the compassion scale. It says, "I'm on board with you."

I believe "pulling up anchor" is another way of saying, "It is what it is," but with a slightly different twist. More like, "You've moved on, and now you're *here*, and I'm right there beside you, to support you." My friend had given me a mental catch-phrase with "pulling up anchor"—one that I immediately threw in my little red wagon—a reminder when listening to others and what they are going through.

My hope is that the next time you are faced with what you perceive to be a crisis, that you see not only the danger, but also the opportunity—that you are able to meet your friend (or yourself), where they are—that you embrace *What IS*. I also hope that you see the blessings as well as the next step in moving forward, even if the next step is to sit quietly and listen to the voice within.

~~~~

"No good sittin' worryin' abou' it," said Hagrid. "What's comin' will come, an' we'll meet it when it does."
~ from Harry Potter and the Goblet of Fire
~~~~

What Do You Own?

Be mindful of what you own.

On September 7, 2011, one week following the three conversations I just shared with you, I stepped out of my car in the pitch black of the wee morning hours, pulled my sweater a little tighter around my shoulders and walked into a Dallas, Texas hospital where a highly skilled and caring medical staff awaited my arrival.

One short month later, while back home standing in my kitchen, this was my experience:

It's all around me, no matter where I look—on almost every commercial, in every store at the mall, on shoes, on billboards, it's even on the football players' jerseys on my son's X-box Live game. But my eggs? Seriously? Yes, when I opened the carton of eggs this morning, I saw a little pink ribbon that had been stamped on top of each and every egg. A clear reminder, in case anyone had forgotten, that October is Breast Cancer Awareness Month.

Minutes later, eggs submerged in a pot of water on the stove, I turned my attention to the stack of mail on the counter as I waited for the perfect, hard-boiled eggs. The first envelope I opened was from a hospital. As I unfolded the contents, I saw that it was a flyer with more of those pink ribbons. Within a border of smallish pink ribbons were dates, times, and titles of upcoming breast cancer events being offered at a Dallas hospital. I remember thinking, *How odd. Why are they sending this flyer to* me? *Hmm.... This must be part of the barrage of pink ribbons I've been seeing everywhere. Or maybe it's just another bill from them.*

At that point, you'd think I would have connected the dots—it's pretty obvious, if I'm getting bills, lots of bills, from a hospital, maybe I'd remember what these bills were actually *for*. For a split second, maybe two, I had completely forgotten that I was the audience they were speaking to! As the foggy film lifted first from my brain, then my eyes, I saw *What IS*: yes, I *was* their target audience. I had been diagnosed with breast cancer—and operated on just one month ago.

Later that day, I mentioned this whole episode to a friend, emphasizing how odd it had felt when I realized the "forgetting and remembering" I had done. I was stunned really, that even for a split second, I would have (could have) forgotten what had recently happened. The fact that I had given pause at all seemed a bit unnatural. I mean, exactly five weeks to the day, hadn't I donned a pale blue hospital gown and been wheeled into surgery, husband and two friends walking beside the gurney as far as the hospital staff would allow?

After listening to me retell my bizarre brain-mind-flip, my friend shared the following story with me:

BRCA 1 and 2

A while back, her sister had gone through the genetic testing commonly referred to as BRCA 1 and BRCA 2—household terms now, thanks to Ms. Angelina Jolie. This genetic testing indicates whether or not a person carries the mutated gene which has been linked to hereditary breast and ovarian cancer. In other words, whether you're predisposed to getting breast or ovarian cancer in the future. It doesn't equate to, *yes you will* or *no you won't*, it simply indicates whether you have the mutated gene. My friend's sister did. (I, by the way, did not.)

She told me that from the time her sister received the positive test results, breast cancer became her identity. Her sister underwent a bilateral mastectomy and became very active in the breast cancer community. She was at every walk, every fund raiser, attended numerous meetings, and the list went on. My friend said it consumed her sister, saying, "My sister completely owned it, and she never even had cancer."

Just to be clear: I'm not suggesting my friend's sister chose a "wrong" stance. I feel confident that all of her volunteer efforts have been very much appreciated. I can only imagine she has formed lasting friendships, raised substantial research money, and contributed to many more positive outcomes.

This is merely an example of how we all handle things differently. Not right, not wrong, but differently. In my opinion, I never owned it. Still don't. I think it comes from a belief system that pulses at my core: *I Am Whole, I Am Healed. I Am Whole, I Am Healed. Whole. Healed.*

To borrow something I heard a woman say while I was in the hospital:

"I wish they hadn't come up with the whole 'I'm a survivor' thing. I feel more like a 'Sur-Thriver!'"

Loving what I had just heard, I thought, *Now that's what I'm talking about!* Let's celebrate surviving such an experience, to be sure, but let's *own thriving* despite it!

So now, I ask you, *What do you own?* Does what you own benefit you? Energize you? Drain you? Define you? And if so, is it your intention to be defined by that particular thing? Maybe the answer is yes. Maybe it's no.

Take a moment and ask yourself these questions. I encourage you to make changes where you see fit, giving yourself a high-five if you confirm you are right where you would like to be. I believe checking-in with yourself from time to time; asking these types of questions will contribute to your *Thriving*.

Again, What do you own?

Learning Through Stillness

You have just witnessed being mindful of what you own is a choice. Similarly, how you choose to learn lessons is a choice. Let me explain.

As a young girl, much of my learning was through crisis—through both danger and opportunity. I remember being thrown into a pool to "learn" how to swim. I learned to fear snakes by having a rattlesnake roam loose in our house. I would hear the rattler at random times throughout the day, petrified it would appear at the exact spot where my seven-year-old body stood: the toy box, the bathtub, around the next corner, behind the closet door, and, of course, under my bed—lurking, waiting for me to let down my guard and move a hair too slowly as I climbed into bed. (To this day, if you hid behind my closet door, you'd witness a hint of a hop on my ascent into bed.)

I learned how to trust by encountering over and over again experiences with people who were untrustworthy.

And I survived it all. I survived it with a sense of truly understanding what trust means.

As the poet Mark Nepo wrote, "While much learning comes from crisis and pain, not all of it needs to. We don't need something to go wrong in order to change."

Wise words from a wise man.

I no longer learn only in times of crisis. I learn in the still moments of life, too. I am able to observe in the quiet spaces between experiencing life's so-called drama.

How do you learn life's lessons? Do you seek the thrill and drama of crisis in order to recognize a learning opportunity? Do you chase that same thrill and drama in order to feel alive? Or are you able to learn in the still, in the quiet, when you are not being driven by adrenaline-induced excitement? Both types of learning are valid, even necessary.

How do you survive life? Has your surviving grown tall, reaching for the sun and the stars, turning into thriving? Remember, the Chinese symbol for crisis combines figures that depict both danger and opportunity. And out of that, comes thriving, the stuff that has you feel your magnificence, your magic.

~~~~

"It's not the load that breaks you down, it's how you carry it." ~ Lena Horne
~~~~

Different, Not Less

I like a slow lifestyle. One that allows for tea sipping and meditation in the early hours of the morning, followed by writing and all the thinking that comes with that territory. Although that's the pace I prefer, having two active boys and simply living in today's world, that's not always the pace I get. There are weeks that sometimes stretch into months when my tea-sipping, life-contemplating dream of a day is exactly that, nothing more than a dream. It was during one of these frenzied periods I began to notice my tank was inching closer and closer to empty. It was time to stop and breathe. This particular Saturday afternoon, I would start refueling with the simple pleasure of watching a movie. No interruptions, no distractions, just me, dog at my feet, cuppa tea warming my hands, and a movie I had been itching to watch for weeks.

Until I interrupted myself.

As the movie began, Claire Danes stepped out as Temple Grandin (the main character of the movie by the same name). Within the first sentence, I knew this was something special. I said *within* the first sentence, not *after* the first sentence, *within* it!

I paused the DVD and popped my head into the playroom. Everyone in my house had to see this! As I hollered for my then nine and twelve-year-old sons to join me, I caught a glimpse of them peering over their shoulders at me, with looks that said, *Are you kidding me? We saw the cover of the movie box, and we are not interested.* Reluctantly, they left their video game, and slower than molasses in January, ambled past me in the direction of the movie, mumbling something unintelligible all the while. My husband paused the golf channel downstairs and gave me "a look" as he approached. Was that his "this had better be good" look or his "I'm humoring you" look? Maybe a little of both.

I was very clear: If, after ten minutes, they weren't thoroughly entertained by Claire Danes and company, they were welcome to leave. Heck, I didn't want them sulking through a movie and ruining my me-time. As it turned out, not a soul left, with the exception of one trip to the bathroom. As my older son made a mad dash for the bathroom, he begged us to pause the movie, to which we all responded with a simultaneous, *"Shhh!!!"*

Meet Temple Grandin

Temple Grandin grew up in a time when we knew very little about autism. Her story is one that is truly amazing, inspirational, and the definition of a "must see" film. I won't give anything away, but do want to share with you something that my older son embraced from the movie in a way that he *owned*—something Temple's favorite teacher said, then her mother repeated, and later Temple echoed herself.

In describing Temple, each said she was, "*Different, yes. Not less.*"

My son liked the way that sounded. Looking over at him in the dark, as he took in the simplicity, yet boldness of those words, I could have sworn I saw him sit a little taller. "Different, yes. Not less."

When you grow up visiting as many doctors as my son has over the years, I imagine you can start to wonder if you're *less than.* Less than perfect? Less than normal? Less than...something your peers are not faced with? By the time he was ten years old, he alone had more "ologists," as he called them, than most families do, distant relatives included. It wasn't until the addition of his hearing aids in the third grade that any hint of teasing occurred. Luckily, it has been kept to a minimum, but with the start of each school year, there is always that one new student who, after noticing my son's hearing aids, inevitably makes an insensitive remark. Something like, "Why do you have those? That's weird. I thought only grandpas and grandmas had those things." At times like those, remembering: "Different, yes. Not less." can serve as a handy mantra.

We Are All Different, Not Less

Here's what I believe: We all have our "thing" (or thingS). Your child may be autistic. He may have ADD, dyslexia, asthma, peanut allergies, warts, be a bed wetter....The list, as you know, is endless. We all have our thing, kids and adults alike.

There are those who deem their particular thing as being better or worse, lesser or more, on some imaginary scale of injustices. But regardless of what our thing is, we have it for a reason. We don't always know the whys and hows of our thing, nor do we need to. See, whatever our thing is, it's there to serve a purpose. We're supposed to experience it, feel it, learn from it—otherwise, we wouldn't have it in the first place. Our thing makes us who we are.

This is where trust comes in. Surely, it's the trust or the knowing that Temple Grandin spoke of when she said, "If I could snap my fingers and become non-autistic, I would not do so. Autism is part of who I am." She owned her autism in a way she was proud of. In a loving way.

There is no resistance to *What IS* in her statement. I hear a person who is embracing who they are and how they were brought into this world. There simply is no fighting *What IS*. Now, that's not to say she didn't fight like the dickens for what she believed, and in most cases, she fought an uphill battle, especially in the profession she chose. But she didn't fight who she was or the condition with which she was labeled. She never gave up. And she never saw herself as less than. Her Will and her Spirit simply could not be broken.

Look at yourself. Look inward. What is your thing? How about your children? Can you discuss your child's thing with them? How does understanding your label, yet not becoming it, not allowing it to define you, differ? How have you been able to compensate? Perhaps even excel? To learn? To grow? And after your learning and growing, how have you shared with others to help them on their journey?

If you're struggling with any of these questions, start with trusting in a higher power. You are not alone. And you are not less. Simply different. No one else comes with your unique gifts and talents to offer the world.

Choices or Abilities?

Some might say Temple Grandin was limited in her abilities. Others would argue that she far exceeded her peers in terms of abilities. But are abilities what really matter here, or as Albus Dumbledore put it, is it more a matter of our choices, Harry?

"It is our choices, Harry, that show what we truly are, far more than our abilities."

I have a secret passion: I love to read out loud to my children. I say secret, because truth be told, I probably do it more for me than for them. Whatever the motivation, it has been wonderful for all of us. One series we adored was the *Harry Potter* series. What an incredible story! The longer I read, the more I became aware of how many details author J.K. Rowling wove throughout the fabric of the story. Something she mentioned in *The Sorcerer's Stone* would show up again in say, *The Goblet of Fire*, then again, at the end of *The Deathly Hallows*. She is a true master of storytelling and deserves every bit of credit she has received over the years!

I cannot think of the *Harry Potter* series without thinking of this quote by Horace Mann:

"Do not think of knocking out another person's brains because he differs in opinion from you. It would be as rational to knock yourself on the head because you differ from yourself ten years ago."

Odd quote for thinking about *Harry Potter,* wouldn't you say? See, ten years prior to reading the series to my boys, I held a very different belief about what these magical books were all about. My belief was that the *Harry Potter* series wasn't suitable literature to read to kids. I held an ignorant notion that it was all about children performing spells on adults. That it was about witches, wizards, dark stuff, foolish stuff. I say ignorant, because I never took the time to ask others, to read reviews, to ground my opinion. I never took the time to *seek.* I simply had an ungrounded belief.

How delighted I am that I opened myself up to *What IS.* What IS are books that are very well written about two topics I find extremely important in the development of one's character. These two topics are Love and Loyalty. The love and loyalty that the main characters display for one another is unmistakable. And a more subtle loyalty, the *loyalty to Self,* is demonstrated time and time again when Harry, landing at various crossroads, chooses to do the right thing, even when it's the more arduous choice.

These books are so well written and involve such depth of character, I easily found myself reading out loud for an hour or more at a time, my boys closely following the plot, eager for more. Despite the fact that these are not small books, their attention was easily held and they followed every detail, pointing out the love and loyalty each time they noticed it.

Had I not opened myself up to *What IS* about this series, I would have missed out on numerous opportunities to share and discuss explicit examples of love and loyalty with my boys. I would have missed out on great vocabulary-building opportunities with them; J.K. Rowling doesn't dummy-down these books. Sure, I could have found other literature with wonderful examples of love, loyalty, and challenging vocabulary, but for me, *I would have missed out on an opportunity to learn from my own closed belief.*

Can you think of any examples where your beliefs differ from yourself ten years ago? Or even differ from yourself at the onset of this book? Specifically, did you believe trust was something you had to earn? Something that someone else had control of, not you? Do you still believe that?

I'm not here to convince you that trust begins from within you. That's not my role. Remember, my role is one of guide, providing stories for those who are interested in learning how to trust.

Part of trusting is being open to new ideas and seeing how (if) they resonate with you. In this example, I'm thrilled I chose to differ from the me of ten years ago, thrilled that I chose to be open to something that before I saw as fatuous. These books not only became something that enriched the lives of my children, but also enhanced our relationship beyond measure. Tender memories were made over the countless hours of sharing *Harry Potter* together, memories that will remain with us throughout our lifetimes.

We all share something in common with Harry: we are all blessed with great abilities. Lucky for you, great abilities come served up with endless choices. And the great thing about choices is there are no wrong ones. If, after choosing something, you see that it doesn't suit you, you reject it, or you simply change your mind, you can always make another choice—one that serves your best interest for where you are in your life at that moment. As Harry would say in that lovely British accent of his, "Brilliant!"

~~~~

We end this chapter by visualizing and tying together the elements that were presented: It is what it is, crisis, different, not less than, what one owns, and choices. In your mind's eye, I'd
~~~~

like you to picture a tiny, rambunctious kitten, literally playing on top of the mouth of a large dog who is lying on the floor. The kitten and dog couldn't be more different.

Do you recognize the two elements from the Chinese symbol for crisis, danger and opportunity, when you imagine the young, innocent kitten and older, fully grown dog? Do you also see something more than danger and opportunity present—a third element? I do. I see trust.

There is trust on the part of the kitten as he plays on the dog's mouth. But more importantly, is the trust displayed by the dog: Trusting *himself* to know he will not harm the kitten.

Perhaps you're thinking the kitten doesn't know any better. He's just along for the ride and whatever happens, happens. I disagree. I don't believe it's part of an animal's nature to automatically trust. Especially not trust the larger animal, at least six times the size and weight, with his big teeth exposed. Animals are driven by a much bigger instinct called *Survival.*

Yet here, in this young kitten's life, a bond has already formed. He feels the warmth and gentleness of the good-natured canine-being he clings to. What could be seen as a crisis is not. It's simply trust. And love, too.

For the dog's part, depending what he was bred for (to hunt, protect, retrieve, etc.), it may or may not be his instinct to harm the kitten. But just by his sheer size and strength, we know he could harm the kitten if he wanted to. So again, what could be seen as a crisis is not. It is what it is: simply trust and love.

As the Chinese symbol expresses: Crisis = Danger + Opportunity

Here's a different word equation I offer you: Trust = Love

And: Love = Trust

An equal sign between trust and love may not be 100 percent accurate, 100 percent of the time, but *What IS* true is this: *Trust and love go hand-in-hand.* That much I know for sure. Trust and love melt away what we may initially perceive as *Different*, as *Less Than*, as a *Crisis*.

Choose trust and love. It is what it is ...beautiful and brilliant!

~~~~

"The best proof of love is trust."
~ Joyce Brothers
~~~~

4

Being Present

"Everything is worship if your mind is focused on the present moment."

~ Paulo Coelho

I can think of no better true life story to share with you to exemplify being present than this one. Please excuse the different writing style—it's still me writing, but I wrote this piece more as an entertainment piece, probably because I get the vague sense that everyone is so tired of hearing, *Be present, practice presence, be in the now*, blah, blah, blah.... When I set out to write this piece, my intention was to share with you a true story, but to share it in such a way as to drive home the importance of being present without boring you to tears. Fingers crossed, wish me luck!

How A Dog Biscuit Saved My Life

I had my first ambulance ride in November of 2012.

Life is so fragile. Everything can change in a split second.

I had been rushing around that morning, running late for a doctor's appointment (only to wait in the lobby for half an hour once I arrived). No matter, I whipped out my iPhone—time for a little catch-up session on Facebook before cracking open my book. And while I'm at it, why not add a status update?

Reflecting on my whirlwind morning, I thumb-typed:

> Dog biscuit in one hand, almonds in the other, rushing to get out of the house to make an appointment on time, I put Libby in her kennel and fed her the almonds as I simultaneously shoved WHAT in my mouth? Yes!
>
> Intention for the rest of the day: I WILL BE PRESENT.

And present I was. Eerily present, as if I had razor sharp senses, yet senses that were balanced with an air of lightness that only a delicate linen scarf could beseech from an elusive wind. And it wasn't just me. For the next seven hours, almost everyone I engaged with appeared to be fully present.

This is where my story begins. Sitting in the waiting room of my doctor's office after publicly declaring my intention for the day: I will be present.

My Story of Presence

"Leslie?" a nurse called out into the sea of smartphone users sitting in the waiting room. I promptly joined her as she escorted me to the surgery room at my dermatologist's office. I was ready to get started! I had a lunch date I had been anticipating for quite some time and I was giddy with excitement! But first, there was a mole to contend with. Ever since I was diagnosed with skin cancer the previous summer, I have a full-body scan every three months. Today I was having a mole on my right shoulder removed due to less-than-stellar pathology results from my recent body scan.

For most, having a mole biopsied or even completely excised is no big deal. However, I come with the fractious problem of being highly allergic to lidocaine, the numbing agent commonly used for this procedure. There are other drugs doctors can use, but all of the ones I've tried come with their own unique set of complications and quirks. (The drug used on me this day was called carbocaine.) For that reason, I've learned to be especially present on excision days. If I'm not, I run the risk of being injected with the wrong drug. This has happened before. Twice.

Being Present

Because of 1) the intention of being present that I had set in the waiting room, and 2) the crapshoot of wondering what was going to happen this time when they injected me, you better believe I was fully present.

Once in the room, I removed my blouse, refusing to put on the barely waist-length, upper-body paper "gown" the nurse was attempting to hand me. "I'm fine in my bra and jeans, thank you. That thing is worthless." As she continued to extend her arm in my direction, holding the fistful of paper gown, she teased, "Oh, come on, they're not that bad."

"You open it then," I responded.

With a quizzical expression on her face, she said, "Sure." As she opened the gown, *R-I-P*, right down the middle.

With my best raised eyebrow gesture (something I've never fully mastered), I threw her a triumphant smile. We both cracked up. "Bra it is!" she said.

Hell-Fire Injections

After thoroughly cleaning my right scapular area with iodine, the Hell-Fire injections began. Hell-Fire because due to my allergy, no buffers are used in numbing agents on me—just straight fire. I squeezed my right hand with my left, hard. Ouch! My teeth! *My teeth?* I assumed I was clenching my teeth because they started to ache almost immediately.

I mentioned this to the nurse, adding, "But why would my front teeth hurt? Wouldn't clenching hurt the back teeth? *Why front teeth?*"

"Hmm? I suppose so," she said. I could tell she really didn't care. I probably wouldn't have either in her shoes. At this point, it was really more like small talk anyway.

Until...holy mother! "Who hit my teeth with a baseball bat?" I screamed.

Things Accelerate

Never, I repeat, never scream when a nurse has a needle in your back.

"Not to worry. All done," she said, with the voice of someone ready to exit quickly, someone who was in the presence of a patient who obviously has a screw loose, who goes from joking about paper gowns to chatting, to screaming oddball things like, *"Who hit my teeth with a baseball bat?"*

I called her by name, a deliberate act to get her attention. "I don't think you understand. Call the doctor now."

She looked at me with the same quizzical look as before, as if she was assessing if this was more of my warped sense of humor. More of the paper gown stuff.

"Now!" I urged.

She got the message.

Peter And His God Complex

In comes, not the doctor, but a different nurse. A male nurse. I'll call him Peter.

Peter proceeded to tell me that there was no possible way I was having an allergic reaction.

"It doesn't work like that," he said. "If you were having a true allergic reaction, it would be localized in the area of the injections. Which were in your back, not your teeth."

Really? They were? As if I hadn't noticed where the Hell-Fire had been injected. Of course I had. I must say, I was extremely present during this entire episode.

"Respectfully, Peter, you are wrong. And if my body reacts to this drug the way it does to lidocaine, it will start to spread to other areas of my body. In under one minute."

Peter leaned in closely, stared into my eyes, quite present himself, and dryly said, "It. Is. Not. Possible," punctuating each word for effect.

Equally flat and forceful, "I. Disagree." Then faster, "I need to see the doctor immediately."

Peter turned to leave. Not bothering to look back at me, he shrugged his shoulders and said, "You can disagree with me all you want. Whatever."

Allergy On The Move

Before the door clicked shut behind him, the extreme pain shot out of my teeth and into the roof of my mouth, then on to my face, ears, and chest. I glanced down at my chest as I struggled to hop off the raised surgery table and saw lobster-red skin I did not recognize.

I bolted for the door and ran into the hallway, not a single care that I was without a shirt. The only person in the hallway was the doctor, sitting in this little alcove-like area, in front of a computer. He was reading something with intense focus.

He looked to his left, saw me, and his face went white.

Unlike normal human speech, I more or less barked, “I need you, Doctor!”

Equally un-human, he barked to no one in particular, “Call 911! Have them send an ambulance!”

Altered Energy

He was by my side in what felt like one giant step. Next, he did something remarkable. In the millisecond it took for him to reach me, he had completely altered his energy. Very calmly, he led me back into the surgery room, lowered the table, and gently sat me down. He began to inhale deeply. Exhale deeply. He nodded his head once, looking me straight in the eye; he wanted me to follow. So I did. Together we inhaled deeply. Then exhaled deeply. Both, never more present.

After a brief period of time, he began asking questions. I answered. We had established a dialogue *around* our breathing. Breathing became our rhythm. It was the foundation, as the questions danced in the periphery.

I heard the rustling sound of fast-approaching, over-starched scrubs and turned my head toward the door. A nurse rushed in, "They're here! Oh! We've got to get you dressed, young lady!"

"No we don't. Send them in. You're distracting me."

She stared.

Eyes back on the doctor. "I'm breathing. Being present. Just show them in."

"But...but...they're EMTs. They're...*men!*"

Looking back at her, I saw men in black uniforms, carrying equipment. Apparently they had found their way to the surgery room, all six of them. I waved them in.

While one EMT asked questions, typing into his laptop, another took my blood pressure, and a third started an IV in my left arm. The other three EMTs stood behind me. Two nurses entered—the woman who had done the injecting and yes, Peter. They also stood behind me, but more off to the side, making them barely visible in my peripheral vision. The doctor remained as close as possible, while staying out of the EMTs' way. We didn't break eye contact as we breathed between responding to questions being directed at us.

We Play a Game

In addition to answering questions, I began to call out where the allergic reaction was moving in my body—I could feel it a millisecond before it would move. For example, I would say, "right shoulder, moving down, stopping at elbow." Within half a second, the area I had just named would turn hot and bright red, for all to see. Next, it was, "other shoulder, moving down, stopping at the elbow." And there it appeared. "Left kidney." "Temples and bridge of my nose." Each time it would appear in the precise location I had named.

This turned into a fun game, albeit somewhat sick entertainment. Still, it was something to pass the time as the doctor and I breathed and the IV drip began to work its magic.

Shifting Moods

Every soul in that room was very present. And for a few minutes the mood even appeared light, or at least it was moving in that direction. There was no delicate linen scarf in the wind just yet—more like the blades of a windmill who had been waiting all night to catch the first morning breeze—waiting, waiting, almost there. A definite sense of growing lightness was in the room; it was within our reach.

Until I said, "Throat."

It's all fun and games until the word 'throat' enters the picture. It was as if J.K. Rowling's dementors had swooped down and begun to work their own magic.

The EMT in charge, the one with the word *Lieutenant* embroidered on his uniform, the one who had just moments before strongly suggested that they transport me to the hospital, and to whom I had told, "No. I don't think that's necessary," gravely said, "Mrs. Green (pause, long enough for two pairs of eyes to lock), you do realize you only have one airway."

"Yes, Brian, lead the way."

Arriving at the ER

I am not a big TV person. I only watch two shows, period. One of them is *Gray's Anatomy* (and the other is *Super Soul Sunday*). Each Thursday evening after I put the boys to bed, I tiptoe down the stairs, rubbing my hands together, thinking, *Ahh, now for a little Derrick and Meredith. A little Christina, Owen, Alex, Arizona, Callie, and Bailey. And just a smidgen of Jackson. Oh, Jackson!* I glance at the clock, making sure enough time has lapsed so I can swiftly fast forward through the commercials. Although I watch Gray's for the people, these actors I could do character studies on in the field of Human Behavior, I also like the backstory. Each time an ambulance pulls up to Seattle Grace (I still haven't warmed up to the new name), I don't wonder what trauma is about to unfold, but instead, I find myself trying to crawl inside the skin of the person on the stretcher, asking myself, *If I were that person, how would I feel? Would I feel anxious? Disoriented? Scared?*

On that afternoon in November, I was that person on the stretcher. And on that afternoon, I felt none of the above. Much to my surprise, I was still quite present. I was greeted by the ER doctor within a few feet of entering the emergency room. When I didn't respond to his first question, he gestured for a nurse to come with blankets. My teeth were chattering and he must have thought I was in shock based on my unresponsiveness. I hadn't been in shock—well, not the way he would classify shock. I was in deep thought, assessing his speech pattern (he had a terribly strong lisp). Old habits die hard; I used to be a speech pathologist years ago.

Embarrassed at myself once I realized what I had been doing, I felt my face turn hot, not that anyone would notice since the allergic reaction had decided to camp out on my face, neck, and ears. Grinning down at me, the EMT gently squeezed my big toe and said, "Look at her. Shivering cold, and a face as red as a tomato!" I smiled at him weakly, wondering if somehow he could see my red beneath my red. Did he somehow know? Was he covering for me? I thought about just coming clean. But what would I say?

No. Instead, I cleared my throat that did not need clearing and began to answer the doctor's questions, probably a little too eagerly, trying to compensate, I suppose. Shortly afterwards, I was wheeled to Room 22. The hours that followed involved the usual: repeated taking of vitals, administering steroids and other medications through the IV, questions, sign here, more questions, sign there, do you have a living will? Power of attorney?...

Approaching night-time, with my airway now fully open, lobster-red skin traded for a shade of medium-to-soft rose, blood pressure back down to normal, sensation having returned to my lips and extremities, I signed one final paper and received the stamp of approval to go home.

Although my airway struggled to remain open for the next three days, which led to more drama than I'd care to remember, this is where my story ends...and yours begins.

Practicing Presence

Sometimes in life we find ourselves in seemingly impossible situations—anxiety-filled situations. Practice being present now, in your day-to-day life, so when you're in a "do-or-die" situation, you can go to that place of presence. The place of calm. Trusting. Breathing.

Advocate For Yourself

So often we don't speak up for ourselves. We're polite when politeness isn't appropriate, when directness is.

1. Show up for yourself by stating your wants (or your don't wants): don't wear the stupid paper gown if you don't want to.
2. Run out into the hallway in your bra and voice your needs out loud: "I need you, Doctor!"
3. Be flexible enough to change your mind once the variables change: "No. I don't think going to the hospital is necessary" to "Lead the way."

Those are examples of advocating for yourself. And they all happen in the present.

This experience, as unpleasant as it was, was bearable *because* I was present. I could have easily freaked out, which I'm positive would not have been in my best interest. By shoving a dog biscuit in my mouth that morning, I set an intention of *being present.* Without that intention of presence, my body could have latched onto alternative coping mechanisms, like going into shock and completely shutting down. (Or worse.)

Life is so fragile. Everything can change in a split second. Set your intention. Declare: I will be present. Better yet, declare: *I am present.*

Get the most out of your beautiful gift called *life.* Set your intention. Be present. Breathe deeply. Live fully. Give thanks.

You are more powerful than you know.

And so are your words.

Strap On Your Seat Belt!

There's no doubt in my mind that you know words are powerful. I bet you could easily recall how you have felt in the present moment when someone looked deeply into your eyes and said, "I love you," or "You are beautiful." Those are moments we all want to be present for. Now, think about the different feelings you've had after either saying or hearing venomous words, versus Truth, versus lies, versus words of compassion.

Before our words are able to affect others, they are thoughts first. Even if they appear to happen simultaneously, there's some force inside us that's at work to push our words out into the atmosphere, allowing them to be heard by another.

Once you say it out loud, it's out there. Period. Good, bad, or indifferent.

At the one-year cancer-free mark, I visited with my former oncologist. He reviewed my chart, looked at my lab work, and asked me a series of questions. When he was done, he turned to me. "Leslie," he said, "I think you have too many doctors in your life. How'd you like to have one less?"

These words were music to my ears!

I was up, out of my seat, shaking his hand,

and out the door before it had time to hit me in the derriere. Talk about being present! That *was* a present!

Although there was never any question in my mind that my meeting with him would go any differently, there was still a certain amount of relief, comfort, and jubilation in hearing his words spoken out loud. His words marked the confirmation to an end of a very different set of words that were spoken out loud by a different doctor, the radiologist who performed my mammogram, the one who called me with the diagnosis while I was at the going-away party, but ended up delivering those words the following morning.

Radiologist's words: beginning. Oncologist's words: ending. Like two bookends, supporting many books in between that were laden with deep lessons. Life lessons would continue, but this book, the c-word book, was closed.

There's something about speaking words out into the air that makes them real in a way they weren't moments earlier while still lodged in our heads. Or even on the tip of our tongues. In the case of awaiting an outcome from a biopsy, these words, after spoken out loud, have the ability to shift an entire mindset from the unknown: *"What IF?"* To the very real known: *"Oh, $@!#."*

It doesn't mean that the condition didn't exist before that moment. But, before life was breathed into the words, it didn't exist to me. It wasn't real, not to the extent that any action had taken place. At the time the diagnosis was delivered, I did not have a breast surgeon, a plastic surgeon, or an oncologist. I had not scheduled any future appointments to interview these specialists. I didn't even know I needed them. After the words were spoken out loud, then the logistics began. Plans started to form. I sat and contemplated how I would take the words the radiologist poured into my ears and syphon them in such a way that they could exit my mouth to create the least possible earthquake when they hit the ears of my husband, my mother, *my kids*. Once the words were breathed into existence, there was no turning back. It was real. The *What IF* faded. No, not faded, it burst like a soap bubble.

Pop! That fast.

This biopsy example is the one I happened to choose, but there are countless others. And they all snap us into being present just as fast as the bursting soap bubble or accidental dog biscuit in the mouth. Everything changes once you hear the words:

- "I'm sorry. We no longer need your services" *or* "Welcome aboard!"
- "Your son has been seriously injured" *or* "Goodnight, Mom. I love you."

- "I want a divorce" *or* "Will you marry me?"
- "Your daughter has a life-threatening disease" *or* "It's a girl!"

Before these words are uttered out loud, they're in the *What IF* category. Or, maybe the non-existent category, not even a part of our conscious thoughts.

Once spoken out loud and made a reality, how you navigate through the two scenarios of *"What IF"* and *"Oh, $@!#"* has a lot to do with where you're operating from at that moment and how present you are. Think about the dog biscuit story from just moments ago. When presented with a seemingly difficult situation, will you choose to view it as a disaster, with all its never-ending *What IFs—What IFs* that morph into insomnia robbing you of sleep, or morph into illness due to a compromised immune system, or morph into irritability with those you love, or just plain irrational thinking? Or will you choose to explore the *What IFs* for a moment (we're all human!), then, without suppressing your emotions, choose to acknowledge your feelings by feeling them fully, being in the present moment, and leaning into the situation, trusting your inner guidance and strength? Trusting you can handle anything Life throws your way?

When Will the Fog Clear?

Being present requires the understanding that there is no such thing as waiting. Yet, you'll see that is exactly what I find myself doing.

I snapped this picture on a bleak, dreary, uninviting January morning in my neighborhood.

As I left the house on this particular morning, surrounded by fog, I thought how much I'd prefer the sun to be shining. How starting a day in the sun is much more uplifting. I even welcome rain over fog. Rain, at least, feeds Mother Earth. That's not to mention how rain provides a good excuse to stay home and tackle projects around the house or get cozy with someone you love.

But fog? I find it a bit evasive, as if it has something to hide. I'd rather the day, *or people*, just show me who they are so we can get on with it!

No matter how much I'd like it to work that way, there are times when the day, or people, do *not* show you who they are. Is it just me, or do you also find yourself feeling confused or empty when you encounter such evasive, fog-like people?

And therein lies my problem: I am not accepting *What IS*.

With the fog, I could wait for it to clear, constantly keeping my focus on the future, wishing for the sun, not appreciating what currently *IS*: *Stillness*.

There is much comfort to be felt in the stillness of the moment. But I wouldn't know that, because I've resigned myself to wait on the sun to appear.

Ah-ha! And there I've caught myself. There is no waiting for the sun. There is no waiting, period. There only exists *What IS*, and in this case, *What IS* is a beautiful stillness. A stillness that will continue for as long as it's meant to.

I am the variable in this situation, not the fog. I am the one who makes the choice: Do I sit, with an anxious desire for the sun to appear? Or do I choose to be present with *What IS?* Do I embrace the stillness and the thickness of the fog, while finding the stillness that resides inside of me? The inner stillness that is peace?

It's like that with people, too. I am the one who makes the choice: Do I sit, with an anxious desire for my friend to see things my way? For it to be my turn to talk? Or do I embrace the stillness—the stillness that exists when you honor the present moment? When you honor the way you believe the universe operates, knowing that everything works out as it's intended?

And maybe, just maybe, while within this stillness, this place of honoring *What IS*, your eyes begin to drift back into focus and you notice the sun has appeared.

Later That Day

How crisp. The blue of the sky is radiant. The air feels clean and fresh. The subtle shadows that are cast from the lampposts reinforce what we already know: Yes, the sun is indeed shining.

Fog, sun, people, circumstances. The choice is yours. Do you choose to sit with anxious desire? Or embrace the stillness of the present moment, believing that in some instances, no action is required.

The act of being will suffice.

Be. Trust in What IS.

What's Normal, Anyway?

No sooner have I embraced *What IS*, relegating myself to the present moment, with the understanding that there is no such thing as waiting, a new day dawns, and with it, so does my practice of remaining present. But I am human, so sometimes I forget.

Didn't I just say there's no such thing as waiting? Yet, as I reflect back on this experience, I clearly remember the feelings of waiting *and* longing. Waiting and longing for my body to feel "normal" again. Waiting and longing for the day that my body would go back to feeling how it did pre-surgeries, pre-cancer.

At the time this story occurred, it had been around eleven months since my first surgery. During that operation, my brilliant surgeons had removed all of my breast tissue and replaced the undesirable tissue with temporary implants (which eventually became permanent implants). Yes, that was eleven months for me to get used to a new body, a new normal. Yet, I still waited, with a slow, somewhat angry irritation simmering at a near boiling point just below the surface of each breath. I could feel the simmer flare each time I got into a yoga posture and found myself stuck there, unable to right my statue-like limbs, waiting for the instructor to notice me and in her sweet, discreet manner, help me up. Of course, my ego was having none of that, so I stopped going to yoga.

But it wasn't just yoga. There was lifting luggage to contend with, closing the hatch on my car, getting a watermelon home from the grocery store (first placing it in the shopping cart, then moving it into my car, and finally bringing it into the house). Each of these tasks required all of my muscle power. Each served as a reminder, a dull whisper that said, "Your body is different. You cannot physically do what you did before. You have limitations." Basically, *things are not the same*. And I didn't like it.

Rationally, I believe that as I grow older these same things would have become difficult for me. But it would have been a gradual process. A process occurring so slowly that perhaps I would have developed methods to compensate on a physical as well as an emotional level.

But that's not *What Was*. That was not my *What IS*.

So I reminded myself, as I've shared with you on numerous occasions, to focus on *What IS*. This is what I came up with:

What IS?

- I am cancer free.
- I am healthy.
- I am stronger emotionally *because* of the experience.
- I have grown spiritually.
- I don't have the upper body strength that I used to.
- I am slowly becoming okay with asking for help, which can make me feel vulnerable.
- I have dead patches under my arms and on my back where the nerves haven't regenerated.
- I let go of the idea that in order to feel normal again, the dead patches must regenerate and produce feeling. If they do, fine. If they don't, fine.

I was inching closer to embracing a new normal.

And I declared that I will be truthful with myself: I would no longer avoid yoga, just because my body couldn't do what it used to.

I will recognize my ego when it shows up, acknowledge it, and refocus on *What IS.*

I will be okay with my best.

Where in your life are you waiting for your new normal? After ending your marriage, are you waiting for your new normal to appear? After moving to a new city, or starting a new job, or losing a big client, or ending a friendship—*where?* Where are you waiting for your new normal?

Your new normal is here. It is upon you. Just as my ever-changing normal is upon me, here, in the present moment. Embrace *What IS*. It's here to teach us something, to serve its purpose, to help us grow as we live the experience. *What IS* is our Truth.

And I trust it.

If you live your life with the understanding of What IS, there is no waiting.

5

The Gift of Surrender

"If we don't change, we don't grow. If we don't grow, we are not really living. Growth demands a temporary surrender of security."

~ Gail Sheehy

Turning Trauma Into Triumph

You were introduced to Trust's Cousin: Surrender, in Chapter 1. Now we explore further.

Perhaps it's because I grew up in a military town that I tend to gravitate toward stories about soldiers who suffer from Post-Traumatic Stress Disorder (PTSD). Or maybe I've been seeing more of these stories lately since our biggest patriotic holiday here in the U.S. just occurred. For whatever reason, I keep running across these stories. And they got me thinking...is there something *beyond* post traumatic? Some sort of benefit that could come from experiencing a trauma?

Could there be such a thing as post traumatic *growth?*

Post Traumatic Growth

First off, who am I talking about here? Who would be considered part of a group who has experienced something traumatic? Since I'm no therapist and don't claim to be an authority on PTSD, I'm going to take it down a notch and not focus on the disorder, but rather focus on trauma in general—*anyone who has experienced a sense of acute anxiety* fits in this category.

And who is that?

Who reading these words has ever witnessed ongoing family violence? Been raped? Sexually abused? Robbed? Attacked? Unfortunately, this list can be quite lengthy. And equally unfortunate, the majority of people reading this right now would raise their hand in affirmation.

So, who in their right mind would associate *trauma to triumph*, as the title suggests?

This is who:

The person who goes through something horrific and *because* of it, comes out stronger. Someone who manages to grow out of the stress and make it to the other side, whole, and intact. And this person, by the way, is also keenly aware of how to appreciate the wonders and beauty of life, because they've experienced the flip side of the coin.

Experiencing the downs makes us appreciate and recognize the ups.

Experiencing the downs gives us the capability to empathize with others.

Experiencing the downs teaches us life skills that lend themselves to traits like tenacity, perseverance, endurance, and intestinal fortitude. These are life skills that we can put in our tool belt—or our little red wagon—and later transfer to other areas of our lives.

Surprisingly enough, there is much good that comes from the down times (sounds less ominous than trauma). In fact, these down times actually prepare us to better handle trauma when it does appear.

Here are some things we have in common:

- We have all had down times.
- Quite a few of us have experienced trauma.
- Reading this book tells me you are seeking Truth.
- If you're a seeker of Truth, then you're strong as hell.
- Strong people like you are strong *because* they've experienced life.
- They're also the people who can turn lemons into lemonade.
- They are people who can turn trauma into triumph.

And these people are you.

You have the ability to turn trauma into triumph in your life. It may not be the easiest thing you've ever done; chances are it'll take some effort. Surrendering to a force larger than you is difficult for many. But I believe you can, and you will.

Start making some lemonade. With the summer heat down here in Texas, I would not turn down a glass if you offered me one! In fact,

I'd be honored to sit and sip lemonade with you. And maybe as we drank, you'd tell me your story of trauma to triumph. You'd tell me of growing more into you through the surrender. You'd realize things about the strength of your character that you didn't even know existed before sharing your story out loud.

With whomever you choose to share your story, you will be helping them learn and grow as they walk through whatever difficult time they may be facing. And by the same loving act of telling your story, you may find yourself growing.

As you surrender, you actively begin to trust. Trust yourself enough to share your story with another. Trust that someone with a piece of you.

A Hole (Whole) In My Heart

Chances are, if you are reading this book, you're of an age where you've experienced heartache. The feelings range from a piercing stab in your heart to a dull murmur that lingers just below the surface of your skin. No matter the intensity or range of the feelings, I believe it's safe to say, we all have experienced what feels like a hole in our heart.

The hole...what *is* that? For me, I believe the hole is a feeling of loss.

While talking to a girlfriend about this very topic—what a hole in your heart feels like—she agreed that it indeed does feel like a loss, a loss of something dear. At this point, I'm guessing some of you may be relating a hole in your heart, and the subsequent feeling of loss, to romantic love or perhaps the loss of a loved one who has passed away. To be honest, while in this conversation with my friend, I was too. Until my friend reminded me of an excerpt from a book I copied and mailed to her over ten years ago. The author had written about his addiction to cigarettes. My friend had been a long-time smoker and had tried to quit, "too many times to count," she admitted. She paralleled the feeling of losing something dear and feeling a hole in her heart to quitting smoking.

Smoking? Yes. I was intrigued. Nice twist—my attention was piqued, which means I was poised to learn.

Going back in time ten years, what I sent my friend was from the book I was reading at the time, *Living to Tell the Tale,* the first volume of Gabriel Garcia Márquez's autobiography. His words made such sense to me, and I thought they might speak to her, too.

Here is the excerpt I mailed my friend:

> Because of the pneumonia I was forbidden to smoke, but I smoked in the bathroom as if hiding from myself. The doctor knew and spoke to me with real seriousness, but I could not obey him.
>
> Already in Sucre, as I tried to read without pause the books I had received, I chain-smoked until I could not bear it, and the more I tried to quit the more I smoked. I smoked four packs a day, I would interrupt meals to smoke, and I burned the sheets because I fell asleep holding a lit cigarette.
>
> The fear of death would wake me at any hour of the night, and only by smoking could I endure it, until I decided I would rather die than stop smoking.
>
> More than twenty years later, when I was married and had children, I was still

> smoking. A doctor who saw my lungs on the screen told me in horror that in two or three years I would not be able to breathe. Terrified, I reached the extreme of sitting for hours and hours without doing anything because I could not read, or listen to music, or talk to friends or enemies without smoking.
>
> One night, during a casual supper in Barcelona, a friend who was a psychiatrist explained to the others that tobacco was perhaps the most difficult addiction to break. I dared ask him what the fundamental reason was, and his reply had a chilling simplicity:
>
> "Because for you, quitting smoking would be like killing someone you love."
>
> It was a sudden burst of clairvoyance. I never knew why and did not want to know, but I put out the cigarette I had just lit in the ashtray, and with no anxiety or regret I never smoked another one again in my life.
> ~ Gabriel Garcia Márquez

A decade later, my friend still remembered these words. When she spoke of it, she said that *quitting smoking feels like losing her best friend.* She would be killing someone she loves. The hole in her heart would feel real and the loss immense. She was not ready to make that surrender.

As Emerson said, "Whenever you meet anyone, remember they are going through a great war." A war where loss is felt. Whether it's the loss of a lover, a parent, a beloved dog, or a habit you've become addicted to, there is real loss there. And in many cases, your heart may feel like it has a gaping hole.

But within that hole, slowly, very slowly, as the ends close and merge from within, the hole you once felt in your heart begins to feel whole again. The key is *from within*. Love yourself from within. Trust yourself from within. Know you are enough, exactly the way you are. *Believe it.*

Surrender. Trust.

And in time, the hole will turn whole again.

How the Heart and Spirit Surrender

"When the heart weeps for what it has lost, the spirit laughs for what it has found." ~ Sufi Proverb

~~~~

With that, our stage is set to investigate our human heart versus our *Spirit*—our intangible, yet very real Spirit.

It's no secret. You know, just as well as any kindergartener, the human heart is associated with love. Beautiful feelings of love. Heart-swelling feelings that are capable of creating magic. Yet at some point after experiencing love, the loss of love will occur—your loved one will pass away, you'll experience a painful break-up. Whatever the circumstance may be, the loss of love will happen and your heart will ache. In the case of our Sufi proverb, *your heart will weep.* I think it's safe to say, the heart-action in this proverb can be seen as: a broken heart, one that weeps out of sadness and a longing to return to a time before the loss, when the heart was still experiencing the blissful, comforting feelings of love.

The heart-half of this proverb is pretty straight forward. But the Spirit-half....
~~~~

Why would the Spirit laugh when the heart weeps?

Here's what I believe:

The heart weeping is a reaction to outside circumstances—your loved one dying, the painful break-up. Weeping is the first overt sign of letting go. Spirit, however, *knows*. There is no action required by Spirit. Spirit is connected with God, Our Creator, the Divine, all that IS. Spirit is not concerned with outside circumstances, because the Spirit sees (knows) the larger picture and rejoices (laughs) in the delight that you are moving through the pain in order to receive the gift that awaits you. By the heart weeping for what it has lost (the loved one, the relationship), the Spirit laughs for what it has gained: the lesson embedded in the bigger picture. The lessons (experiences) that will in due time, serve you in incredible ways as you maneuver through Life.

The blessing in these lessons will set you free.

These sorts of lessons are huge. They are why we share with one another: to learn from one another—and ultimately, to grow. The Spirit knows how important the lessons are for learning and growing, and for that reason, it laughs. It rejoices at the very moment the heart weeps.

As you learn to surrender, remember, you are learning to trust (flow) with the currents of your life. Surrendering to a force larger than you is not giving up. By listening to your heart, you are leaning into love. Which is to say, you are trusting in the Divine.

Scratch That Itch

I am not one to ask for help. I used to think this was a strong, noble, honorable trait. I now see it for what it is: a glaring flaw in my personality—nothing more than my ego jumping in the driver's seat, not wanting myself to be seen as vulnerable. This vulnerability I've tried so hard to hide from the world became especially hard to cover up while in the hospital. I remember waking up from the first surgery, still in the recovery room, and trying to reach up to scratch my nose with my left hand. Not only were there cumbersome wires impeding my reach, but I literally couldn't scratch my nose. I was still so drugged up I couldn't move my arm in an upward motion, let alone employ the type of dexterity involved in wiggling my index finger to scratch. But my nose itched. It really itched. So I thought, maybe if I try with my right hand I'll have more luck; there were fewer wires on that side. Nope. I couldn't raise either arm. Both arms felt as if they were buried under a vat of thick, dense cement that had already begun to set; there was no way they were budging, not even a centimeter, much less all the way to my nose.

At that point I considered asking the nurse to scratch my nose for me. Then I thought better. She had much more important things to do. But

I'm telling you, it *really* itched. So, I opened my mouth to make what was beginning to seem a half-desperate, half-ridiculous request, and nothing came out. I couldn't talk—no sound, not even a whisper.

To get her attention, I decided to move my head from side to side, as if to say, "No," and sure enough, she looked over at me. As she stood over me, inquisitive look on her round, sweet, face, she tried to understand what I was attempting to communicate by scrunching up my nose. It was futile. So I changed my mind and simply smiled at her, feeling my dry lips tight, on the verge of cracking. In that instant, I decided that there were going to be many small things I wouldn't be able to do for myself while recovering. Some of them would be tolerable and some of them would not. This one was tolerable, so it wasn't worth straining further. And of course, as soon as I let go of the urgency for my nose to be scratched, as soon as I surrendered, wouldn't you know, it stopped itching.

The following day I was told by a different nurse that my catheter was going to be removed and I would have to walk to the bathroom. At the time I remember thinking I hadn't heard her correctly. Yesterday I couldn't scratch my nose, and today, she wanted me to *walk* to the bathroom? I wasn't annoyed or even disagreeable, I simply chuckled inwardly, thinking, "Yeah, right. *That is NOT happening.*"

The next thing I knew, she said, "Breathe out hard on three. One, two, *three.*" She had removed the catheter (on three) and said she'd be right back to help me to the bathroom. I had heard her correctly. It was beginning to sink in. This really was going to happen. In a few moments she expected me to walk to the bathroom. Walk. *But how?*

Minutes later, with my husband on my left side holding me up, and the nurse-of-doom on my right, holding the other arm, they very slowly hoisted me out of bed and held on tightly as I shuffled my way to the bathroom—approximately six feet away. I believe it took a full ten minutes to walk those six feet, but I made it.

Once in the restroom I had a sudden urge to brush my teeth. To my surprise, I couldn't unscrew the top off of the toothpaste. I simply didn't have the strength nor the fine motor skills to master it. As if a bucket of ice water had been squarely thrown in my face, all at once I knew: I needed help, and a lot of it.

For a long time I had been writing about letting go and surrendering. Intellectually it made perfect sense. This, however, was a tangible surrender. One that I couldn't learn from reading a book or from listening to another person's story, but one I had to experience on my own.

So I surrendered. I allowed everyone around me to help in any way possible. And you know what I learned? I realized that when you need h-elp, especially when you're experiencing a physical aliment, others around you want to help, but often they don't know what to do. However, if you allow them to help, if you allow yourself to become vulnerable and ask for their help, they become part of the healing process and that's where the beauty occurs. Magic really.

Look around, allow someone to help you. Then watch your bond with that person grow. Through the growth, your human connection with another strengthens. Each of us grows through exposing our vulnerabilities, by trusting ourselves enough to show another our weaknesses and knowing (believing) that through it all, they will still love us.

The Art of Crashing

Think back to years gone by, back to when you learned how to ride a bike. Do you have it fixed in your memory? Now, think back to the inevitable crash that followed. It happened to the best of us. Maybe years later, at some point in your life, you repeated the crash on a skateboard, on rollerblades, on skis, on a surfboard—or all of the above!

I've experienced many types of crashes in my life, but never on a surfboard. While I openly declare I'm no surfing authority, I cannot help but notice the grace and skill surfers demonstrate. With no apparent effort I can detect, they mount their boards—boards we know are utterly unstable. They negotiate waves of all sizes with more ease than I can manage to prepare a simple peanut butter and jelly sandwich. And have you ever watched them wipe out? There's no flailing about. No out-of-control appearance of their extremities. Just one fluid movement as they hit the water—more like, glide into the water. It's as if in the moment of the mishap, they have already let go, already surrendered, and are now managing to crash with style. How is it they look so graceful while crashing so hard? At such speed?

These are the sorts of things I wonder about.

Here's what I decided: There must be an art to crashing.

I imagine instinctively, their arms ascend slightly upwards, ready to protect their heads. (There will be no flailing going on.) I also guess that along with not getting knocked out, a main area of focus is on how to quickly get to the surface for air.

After that, what more is there? (If you are a surfer, I apologize—I am absolutely positive I'm way oversimplifying this.)

Now, let's assume the surfer isn't injured. We'll agree that with the fall, what the surfer was attempting to do didn't turn out the way he/she had planned; they may even call it a failure. So, what have they gained?

Knowledge.

Knowledge on how to:

- stay up longer
- maintain focus
- better maneuver the waves
- fall with grace—not for the sake of grace itself, but for the sake of survival

And all of this encompasses: The art of crashing, surrendering to a force larger than oneself.

Without the crash, where does the knowledge come from? Reading a *Surfing For Dummies* book? Watching YouTube videos on surf boarding? While not bad ideas, the art of crashing provides the firsthand knowledge that leads to the goal of how to stay up longer, how to maintain focus, how to better maneuver the waves.

After the Crash

How many times in life do we fall? Fail? How many times do we crash? And after that fall, failure, crash, how often do we decide it's just not worth it? *I won't love again because I don't want to get my heart broken.* (Crash.) *I won't attempt to let anyone see the real me because I don't want to be betrayed again.* (Crash.) *I cannot trust because....* (Crash.)

The broken heart, the betrayal, the inability to trust, those are the crash. Why not choose to be the surfer who crashes with grace? Not for the sake of grace itself, but for the sake of survival. Your survival. And after your survival is realized, and you know you've reached the top of the water, and that yes, you are indeed inhaling the beautiful oxygen now filling your lungs, continue to push forward. Ask yourself what knowledge was gleaned by living through this experience? What lessons were learned?

There is a definite art to the crash. It thrusts us forward and helps us heal as we take what we've learned to mend the broken heart. To allow others to see the real us. To trust.

I encourage you to look for the surfer within. Examine your crashes and be open to the lessons and experiences they reveal.

Think of Trusting Life as a spiritual law. We must step back and allow it to work—that's part of the art of it, part of the surrender. When we worry, over-think a situation, hold grudges, and so on, we interrupt the flow. It's through listening, becoming aware, letting go, surrendering, and accepting *What IS* that we're able to Trust Life.

Trust begins inside of you and radiates outward.

Feel, Know, Believe that you are taken care of. You are never alone. There is a bigger force, a bigger plan that you are unaware of. Trust.

6

Finding Your Inner Strength

"A woman is like a tea bag—
you never know how strong she is
until she gets in hot water."
~ Eleanor Roosevelt

Toward the beginning of this book I mentioned *you were powerful, powerful, powerful.* It's true. You are stronger and more powerful than you know.

First, part of recognizing your inner strength is knowing how to see the flip side—recognizing when you are depleted. Often we run around, purely functioning on what amounts to exhaust fumes. In these times, it's important to notice what's happening and stop to refuel.

Wilted and Parched

The weekend before I disclosed on my blog that I had been diagnosed with breast cancer, I decided to have a little girl-time with a close friend. No kids, no schedule, no demands, no nothin'.

When I arrived at my girlfriend's house to begin our no-demand weekend, Kelli was standing in her kitchen, in the process of bringing a plant back to life. As she gingerly placed the off-green looking crumple in her kitchen sink, she called me over to look at its sad, sad state—wilted and parched. As she drenched it in water, she was quite convinced that it would revive and resume its beautiful state, finding its inner strength.

I had my doubts. A few hours later, she had her doubts, too.

There have been times in my life when I have felt wilted and parched. As if no amount of rest or sleep could plump my skin or satisfy my thirst.

Busy Doing, Doing, Doing

During my teens and twenties I didn't realize when I was feeling depleted, so I would just plow forward. The more I pushed through, ignoring the warning signs my body was giving me, the more depleted I became until finally I'd come down with a cold or strep throat or something that would force me into bed to rest. I remember one time I had neglected myself so, I wasn't able to walk more than a few feet without sitting down. As this persisted over several hours, my husband became concerned and took me to the hospital. They immediately hooked me up to an IV—I had been so busy doing, doing, doing, I had neglected my basic need for water. I was severely dehydrated, just like my friend's plant. All inner strength had vanished.

Our immune systems become weak the more we tax them. Lack of sleep, improper diet, repeatedly exposing ourselves to negative thoughts, all of these have an impact on our physical bodies.

Wilted and parched.

The answer was so simple: Stop. Rest. Breathe. Drink some water. Engage in activities that feed my spirit. And although the answer was simple, I'm embarrassed to say it took me years to learn the lesson Life kept trying to teach me.

Austin, Texas

Before taking this girls' weekend, I had started to sense the slowly rising need to recharge my battery. It's incredible what a weekend of Amy's Ice Cream, sipping tea and chatting, eating tacos stuffed with *carnitas*, having zero demands on me or my time, and a pitcher of sangria on a hot July afternoon in Austin, Texas, can do.

On a similar hot July day, seventeen years earlier, my mother-in-law pulled me aside on her patio and shared this bit of advice with me, "Make sure things are right with Mother *first*. If things are right with Mother, things will be right in your house."

Although I wasn't a mother yet, I knew what she meant. I saw the house she referred to as something both concrete, the traditional noun, but also an intangible house, more like the temple where body and spirit reside.

On the last morning of my girls' weekend, I remember looking over at my friend's plant as I sat sipping tea; Kelli still peacefully sleeping.

Although the plant took several more hours to revive than either of us had anticipated, it had indeed perked back to life. It had been sorely wilted and parched.

Allow the Light In

That weekend was a nice kick start. But like the plant, who took easily twice as long to perk up this time around, I had more replenishing to do. The good thing about a cancer diagnosis is it forces you to stop, slow down, evaluate in a sobering way *What IS*, and in my case, immediately begin the healing process. I dedicated every waking moment, and set the intention for every sleeping moment, to feed my spirit. To grow my inner strength. To allow the light in. And to honor the light within by being still enough to feel its shine.

Begin now! Don't wait for Life to deliver some news that forces you to love yourself enough to care for yourself. Stop right now and do an energy check. How do you feel? Are you right on track? If so, great! Are you running a little low on energy? A lot low on energy? That's okay—you are now aware. Start to feed your spirit now. The biggest part of slowing down and feeding your spirit is taking the time each day to love yourself. What does that look like for you?

Is it loving yourself enough to take a nap? Loving yourself enough to kick up your heels and have some fun? Read a book? Go out for ice cream? You may feel inclined to beat yourself up for becoming depleted in the first place, telling yourself things like, *I know better than that.* Relax. You're human. The key is to love yourself, while acknowledging both your shadow side, as well as your sunshine.

Let me explain.

Yin, Yang, Sunshine, and Shadows

"In Asian philosophy, the concept of **yin yang**, which is often referred to in the West as 'yin and yang,' is used to describe how polar opposites or seemingly contrary forces are interconnected and interdependent in the natural world, and how they give rise to each other in turn."
~ Wikipedia

Think about that for a moment.... It's not just that two forces are seemingly opposite (take night and day for example) it's that they are *interconnected* and *interdependent*, each giving rise to the other. You can think of them as *complementary opposites*.

In the days preceding my surgery for the double mastectomy, I had a strong urge to be surrounded by nature. The thought of a sterile hospital room gave rise to dreams of breathing in lung-full after lung-full of fresh, mountain air. The stifling heat of Dallas in August and the flat landscape of home was no such place. So my husband surprised me, and we flew to Seattle, Washington. He knew I wanted to be somewhere that was new and different, a place to take my mind off what was coming. A place I could hike and be with nature, see verdant foliage, cascading waterfalls, and use my soon to be bed-bound muscles to hike as I breathed in the trees.

On our second day in Seattle, we met up with a girlfriend of mine and her sweet dog. We hiked at a place called Twin Falls. Imagine a forest scene, with thriving vegetation as well as barren, desolate spots. Picture the shadows and the sunlight. See a stream of water as well as arid patches. Notice all the opposites. Now, with your senses, reach for a place of balance—of yin and yang.

Later, back in Dallas, and after leaving the hospital, my emotions would remind me on a daily basis of that hike with all of its opposites. There were days I felt as if the whole of the world was made of sunshine, shining rays of cancer-free sunlight directly down on me. I felt as if my cells were thriving and there was a stream of life flowing through me that was unstoppable.

Then, there were days when shadows crept in, arid patches made themselves known, and desolate thoughts appeared. Those were days when I may have felt particularly sore and wanted more pain killers, or perhaps I was running low on energy because I hadn't yet found a comfortable way to sleep.

Understanding the balance of yin and yang, understanding their interconnectedness, reminded me to honor both the sunlight and the shadows.

We're so often told to look at the bright side, to focus on the positive. And I for one, agree. I do these things in my daily life, as I'm sure you do, too. However, we're often not given the counter message: to acknowledge the not-so-bright side. By sweeping whatever the not-so-bright side is under the rug and pretending it doesn't exist, we are in essence throwing off the balance (in this case, the yin) and therefore not accepting all of what truly *IS*.

Are there shadowy areas in your life you're not acknowledging? Is it easier to sweep certain things under the rug? Let me be clear, I'm not suggesting you dwell here in this space; what I'm suggesting is that you acknowledge both the yin (the shadow) and the yang (the sunshine).

By honoring both, you allow yourself to feel *What IS*. Why is it so important to feel *What IS*? Because in order to let go and surrender, in order to build your inner strength, you must first acknowledge the truth of a situation. The truth resides in *What IS*.

Goofy-Juice or Confidence?

No parent looks forward to their child going into surgery. True, the surgery may be necessary and you may feel in your heart that it's the right thing to do for your child, but the pure act of *going into surgery* is a bit unnerving.

Each time my son has been wheeled away on the hospital bed, I've stood and watched his head grow smaller and smaller as he leaves my side, being carted down the hallway, until finally they turn a corner, out of sight. Last week was no different.

It begins the same every time. Doctor's appointments, followed by more appointments, more assessing, until finally I hear these words, "Mr. and Mrs. Green, at this point, surgery is the best option for your son." Then comes the pre-op appointment, followed by the call from the anesthesiologist the night before surgery to review his medical history and details regarding any adverse reaction he may have had in the past to general anesthesia.

This time we had a slight variation. The anesthesiologist said that based on my son's age, he could now make some of his own decisions.

"Really? What sorts of decisions?"

She asked me to discuss two things with him after we got off the phone:

1. Would my son prefer the IV started while he's awake or after he has been put to sleep with the mask? (Mask—no brainer. I know my kid, but I asked anyway.)

2. Would he like some "goofy-juice" before he goes into surgery to ease any anxiety he may be feeling?

(Goofy-juice is this nasty looking liquid they offer him after he has put on his gown, but before they wheel him away. It's supposed to calm the nerves.)

Hmm.... This one was not a no brainer. See, I've observed my son over the years and I've noticed that with each surgery his level of anxiety beforehand has increased. To my surprise, before his last surgery, he had opted for the goofy-juice for the first time. Maybe he'd want it again.

So I asked.

And he silently thought.

After about a minute, he looked up at me and said, "I don't know, Mom. Have them ask me tomorrow morning when we get there. I'll decide then if I'll go with goofy-juice or confidence."

Well, okay then.

As he ran off to take one final dip in the pool (before it became off limits), I thought, *Wow. Goofy-Juice or Confidence.* I had asked him a question: Do you want the stuff or not, never mentioning the word *confidence*, never alluding that there were additional options to consider; it was a simple yes/no question in my mind. Yet he automatically created a different way of saying *no* to the goofy-juice, and he had assigned it the label of Confidence.

What Is Your Goofy-Juice?

When you're faced with a stressful situation, or you feel your anxiety begin to rise, what method/thing do you use to take the edge off? It can be anything that helps to relax your mind, your body, your Self.

After some self-reflection on this question, I decided to ask a few people what their goofy-juice was. Here are some of the responses I received:

- wine
- watching TV
- shopping
- eating
- sex
- yoga
- reading a book
- meditating
- calling a friend on the phone
- watching a comedy

- taking a shower
- going for a run/working out
- walking the dog

I'd say that's quite a list, considering I only asked a few people.

Look over the list again. Try not to slot anything into a "Good" or "Bad" column, and remember the yin and yang?—it's all a matter of balance. As long as that balance exists, couldn't each and every one of the items on the list serve you well, provided you're not running with a broken ankle or something like that?

When To Say When

It's when we begin with a glass of wine, then drink the entire bottle, then the second.... It's when we turn the TV on and stare at it for hours, while mindlessly grazing on a bag of Ruffles (oh, yes, we can definitely mix and match from our list). It's when we do anything to the extent that we numb ourselves.

And it's also when we don't see things like Confidence as an option. We ignore such things as Confidence and Courage altogether. Maybe because Confidence and Courage aren't things we *do*, they are characteristics we *possess*. Does that mean we can't add them to our list? Of course not!

1. Create your own list. Use the one above as a springboard. Add or subtract, making sure to include traits you *possess*, as well as things you *do*.

2. Now, with list in hand, become aware of what your goofy-juice-of-choice is.

3. Then ask yourself: Does my goofy-juice serve me well?

If you responded, "Yes": then great! Keep it up, Brother! Keep it up, Sister!

If you responded, "Well, my goofy-juice kind of serves me well": then ask yourself, *What can I switch around?*

- Maybe add more opportunities to laugh in your life.
- Maybe take away talking to friend after friend about what's bothering you. Focus on one friend. Someone who's a straight shooter, who speaks your language and will be honest with you.
- Tweak away!

If you responded, "No, my goofy-juice does not serve me well at all", then:

- Know that your goofy-juice-of-choice is probably lacking any juice at all; it may be all poison, using sugar as its sweetening mask.
- Don't worry—Now you are aware of it.
- Once you're aware, you can do something about it! That's gotta feel good, knowing you can do something about it.

Look back at your list, think of it as an inviting menu you can choose from. And because you've done this exercise, you'll know what to order as soon as you feel any anxiety begin to present itself.

(And because I know you'll wonder if I don't mention it, I'll go ahead and tell you that my son chose confidence over the goofy-juice that morning. But here's the thing, this is very important: I hope he *only* chose confidence because that's what he personally needed that day, at that time in his life. I hope he always keeps his options open and chooses what serves him best, knowing he can change his mind, knowing that loving himself first is the key to making solid decisions for his higher good and for feeding his inner strength. Knowing. Believing.)

Know yourself. Know your needs. And love yourself enough to make the right choices for *you*.

Broken Places

With each surgery my son has endured, with each loss you have experienced—the loss of a loved one, the loss of a job, the loss of Self through numerous acts, I have to believe Ernest Hemingway was right when he said:

"The world breaks everyone, and afterward, some are stronger at the broken places."

This is not true for everything. Take inanimate objects, they break all the time. Some we wouldn't even consider trying to fix. Imagine you dropped a light bulb and it shattered in a million tiny slivers and shards of glass. You wouldn't dare try and fix that. Why bother? How about an eggshell? After cracking open an egg, would you consider trying to fix it? Of course not. I think we'd all agree that there are some things we wouldn't attempt to mend, bind, glue, or otherwise repair at all.

However, this is not the case with humans.

How is this so? How is it that in our humanness, we can withstand being broken? Broken hearts, broken spirits, just plain broken...*yet we mend.* And often times, we mend stronger in precisely the places we were broken.

By the mere nature of being human, we are resilient. We adapt. We rebuild. And those of us who are fortunate, as we gather our broken bits, learn all the while—making us stronger in those exact areas.

Here's a true story, one I think many can relate to. In high school, I was crazy about this guy. Long story short, he broke my heart, or so I thought. After a few weeks (or was it months?) of feeling sad and broken, a blessing occurred; I call it "flipping the light switch."

Nothing prompted the light switch to flip. I mean, I wasn't trying to solve any problem or figure anything out, it just flipped. The feelings of sadness and being broken evaporated completely. And that day, as the switch flipped inside me, I knew that my boyfriend hadn't really broken my heart; he hadn't done anything *to* me at all.

I had been misdirecting my energy. It was as simple as that.

The light switch, as I've come to know it, is Truth. The truth was he had been in my life for a reason, the relationship ended, I experienced what I was intended to, and I learned from it. I learned to recognize and own my part in the demise of the relationship (*mend*). I learned that going forward I would allow certain behaviors in my partners and not allow others (*mend, mend*). And I'm happy to say that since learning these lessons, little to no mending has been necessary after subsequent breakups. Talk about growing inner strength!

I was indeed stronger in the places I had been broken.

Whether it's a broken heart, a broken spirit, or broken trust, remember these words, "...and afterward, *some* are stronger at the broken places."

Are you the *some* Hemingway was referring to? If not, what would it take to cause a shift so you too can be stronger at the broken places? Because the breaks will happen.

If you find yourself struggling with this, breathe into it. Your light switch will flip when you're ready to receive the blessing.

In the meantime, trust.

7

Letting Go

"Getting over a painful experience is much like crossing monkey bars. You have to let go at some point in order to move forward."

~ C.S. Lewis

Even as I write this book, still in manuscript form, I feel the weight of this chapter—letting go is no small thing. The common religious word for letting go is *forgiveness*, and as you know, is the key to so much. That said, I've never met anyone who has claimed to have mastered letting go. If we're lucky, we have glimpses of mastery, but for the ordinary non-Christ, non-Buddha human, letting go is a daily practice. Once you learn to let go, you are able to surrender and form your foundation of trust. You will gain the peace that we all so desire.

The concept of letting go isn't difficult to understand. It's the *how* that drives us nuts. There's just one way to approach letting go: Dive in with me! (Warning: letting go is not for wimps.)

The Window Beyond

"I'm so angry I could kill him. And to think, that was over two years ago. If he walked in that door right now, I swear..." she stared into her coffee, absentmindedly adding another sugar packet. That made four. I wondered if she was even aware.

Her sister, or was it her friend—same hazel eyes, same heart-shaped face—leaned in to say something, then scooted back in her chair, closed her eyes, and made the smallest sideways movement of her head, as if to say, no, never mind.

Glancing up from her sugar with coffee, "What? Say it."

The sister-friend hesitated, "If only you could just let go. He let go of you a long time ago."

"*Let go?* If I only knew how!" And with that, she flung her chair back, grabbed her purse and scarf, and headed toward the front door. Sister-friend rushed behind, half-worry, half-embarrassment on her face.

Breaking Out of Jail

Does any of this sound familiar? Have you, similar to the girl above, ever constructed your own self-made prison?

Have you ever:

- Held a long-term grudge?
- Resented someone deeply? Mildly?
- Felt self-righteous because of what someone else did to you?
- Lashed back at someone?
- Deliberately chosen not to forgive someone?
- Thought of ways to get even?

I'm not talking about plots so sinister they'd actually land you in jail; I'm talking about the everyday stuff we do when we think we're protecting ourselves—by using our so-called defense mechanisms. As long as I hold this grudge, then I'm protecting myself. As long as I don't forgive you, then I'm protecting myself. As long as I somehow avenge what you did to me, then I'm protecting myself.

Now who's in prison? I am. The person who won't let go.

I call this: The prison of self-righteous resentment.

In the prison of self-righteous resentment, we get to be right. Woo-hoo! (Said with flat, dry sarcasm.) Along with being right, we get to be unhappy, angry, bitter, and frustrated. As a bonus, we have the displeasure of reliving the infraction over and over as it bounces around in our minds, more active than a pinball machine gone haywire.

But we also get a catchy story to tell! One that's interesting. And exciting. Full of drama, action, and suspense. One that gets us lots of attention. People stop to watch the aftermath of a car wreck, don't they?

Stop your drama. You are the car wreck they're stopping to watch.

And as long as you are the car wreck, you're also the one remaining not-so-nice and cozy...in your self-made prison.

Here's the good news:

You Have the Key

The cell you've fashioned may feel more airtight than any chamber you can imagine in the dankest, darkest dungeon, but turn around. Look for the light, no matter how small it is, streaming through the keyhole, there is light. *And you have the key.*

(Or the slippers, Dorothy. You've had them all along.)

Use your key: Trust yourself. Act on that trust, believing you are strong (powerful) enough to relinquish the grudge. You're strong (powerful) enough to work through your resentment. You're strong (powerful) enough to forgive. Because each one of these acts is for the good of you—your health, your well-being, your concentration at work, your even temperament with your children, your sleep at night, your inner peace.

It's for the good of you. And it starts with you, *within* you. There's no need for breaking out of jail—you hold the key. Use it and walk out, into the light and life that await you. Free yourself.

Back in the cafe, at an adjacent table, I watched as two cups of barely touched coffee, one with a sunken sugar treasure, were collected and taken away. Now, with no angry and somber faces seated directly in front of me, my eyes drifted to the window beyond.

Directly outside the cafe window stood a tree with only a few leaves on its branches. A tree, "*let go*," just beyond the window, few leaves, "*he let go of you a long time...*", leaves hanging limply one moment, parallel to the ground the next—strong wind. "*If I only knew how!*" Clearly, a storm was approaching. Content to be on this side of the window, hands wrapped around my Earl Grey, I sat perfectly still, staring at the leaves. "*Let go. He let go of....*" Leaves that held on so tightly. Not a single one relented its grip, not even with such wind.

And then I remembered.

A Tale of Letting Go

> On a still day last week, I was looking out my window, yellow Lab at my feet, just as yours is now I'm sure. (He was right. She was.) The remaining leaves on a nearby tree were dropping, kind of like feathers dropping. I leaned into that and I listened by giving my full attention to them. What they began to say to me, not in words, but in their very existence and how they were falling, was

> they were just letting go. They were just letting go and drifting to the earth.
>
> And amazingly, they had held on through all the storms of this fall. None of all that rough and tough and turbulence took them down. And after that, on a quiet, still day, in silence, they just let go.
>
> The reward for holding on is, at some point, we just let go.

That is the story of listening and letting go that Mark Nepo shared with me on the phone one afternoon, as I interviewed him for his new book, *Seven Thousand Ways to Listen*. His was a tale of listening by giving his full attention to the message nature was delivering. A message of holding on and of letting go.

If I Only Knew How!

If only the girl knew how to let go. If only we all knew how to let go. If only, after weathering years of all sorts of storms, we could, on a quiet, still day in silence, just let go. If only we could be those leaves. But no. Instead we try (and fail) to let go by ignoring. By denying. By repressing. By making believe. By, by, by.... Letting go will never work like that. To let go of something, we first must acknowledge and admit it. (Admit what? Admit *What IS.*)

But wait—ignoring is easier, so is denying. Making believe and blaming—yes, blaming (I forgot to mention that one earlier)—those can even be fun. Addicting.

To be read in a whisper: *But admitting he has moved on without me?* Hush, keep quiet now, that way no one will hear how badly it stings to admit. So instead of letting go, we hold on a bit longer. A bit tighter.

But all we're really holding onto is our pain. Pain that we are, in effect, prolonging. If you're ready to be free of pain and truly want to let go of anger and resentment, start by admitting the truth of a situation.

For the first year my blog was active, I focused on establishing my voice, trying different methods until I discovered how to connect on the internet. No matter how many times I switched things up, two things remained the same: 1) my slogan: "Let Go...Trust Life" and 2) the quote on the home page by Hermann Hesse:

> *"Some of us think holding on makes us strong, but sometimes it is letting go."*

I've come to think of that quote as my own personal "Trust Life Today" quote. And although it's no longer on my homepage, I love the Hesse quote so much I've had it printed on just about everything—business cards, stationery, postcards, notepads, and even on various Trust Life Today products. It simply speaks to me. I hope it speaks to you, too. Holding on is important. Not giving up, being tenacious, seeing things through, these are all honorable and important. Equally important in honoring yourself is knowing when to let go. When to say when.

Letting go makes up a major part of my life philosophy. It is sandwiched right there between Trust and Peace. So much so, that I had a custom-made necklace to reflect the three. A trilogy of sorts.

The three have become my personal formula:

By learning to *Trust Life (each) Today*—we are able to *Let Go*—which leads to what I believe we seek most: *Peace*.

This is not only a formula, it is a daily practice.

The more we hold on, the more we're weighed down. You say you want to move forward in your life? Well, yes, I do too. So, let's begin by letting go of all that doesn't feed our present well-being. The past is done, the future is still developing.

Look to the window beyond. Let go and trust that a greater outcome is already yours.

Before You Officially *Lose It*

Items to let go of come in all sizes. There are the small annoyances, like the person sitting next to you chomping on their ice. Or the clerk who is more interested in her texting marathon than helping you find the last item on your shopping list. Then there are the elephant-sized *let go's*, things like not being acknowledged or listened to when you are hurting or leftover feelings of abandonment from your childhood.

The more we practice letting go and trusting life with the small stuff, the better prepared we are to handle and eventually let go of the larger life events that tend to knock us off our feet. In other words, learning to let go of the daily, smaller things will make available the mental space needed to dedicate to the larger ones.

Swatting at Gnats

Often we have so many small "let go's" hovering around us, we tend to leave them unaddressed. Our tendency is to spend all of our energy and effort shooing away these smaller items, never really addressing them or resolving anything. While constantly having our focus *out there* (yet, nowhere in particular), it feels as if we're swatting at gnats; we never allow ourselves to delve into what's at the root—the feeling in our hearts, or the forgiveness we've been meaning to get around to—until some small little something happens, and we experience the big, ugly SNAP. That snap that comes when you have officially lost it!

By the time we lose it, we're exhausted, frustrated, and entirely depleted, although we have no idea why we're feeling this way. We wonder why such a little something made us lose our heads. In reality, it wasn't the little something at all. The fact that we didn't pause long enough to consider all of the minutiae we weren't dealing with is what led to the big, ugly snap. We were drained of our energy and lashed out in a way that felt uncontrollable at the time. That's when you might hear yourself say, "I don't know what came over me. That's really not like me at all."

By not acknowledging and not letting go of the smaller items as they arose, you essentially created a scattered space from which to operate. From this standpoint, you lacked the tools to handle more incoming items, especially the larger ones. So, when one of these larger items does present itself, you wonder: *Why can't I just let this go? Why can't I forgive her? Why am I having such difficulty getting over this?*

Learning how to let go of the smaller items as they occur helps us on so many levels:

- We are better able to be present in our daily lives.
- We have the mental space available for the larger "let go's."
- We are more prepared to let go of the larger items because we've practiced, hopefully on a daily basis, with the smaller ones.

Once you clear all of that space and regain your energy, what happens? You begin to focus on Life. And living it to the fullest. You begin to sleep better at night. You begin to feel peace. Joy. Happiness.

The key is to start small. Practice letting go *daily*. Grow that muscle until you're ready for the larger "let go's."

Honoring Life

Here is a story of a family I observed in the practice of letting go. They were focused on life, even in the face of death.

On a beautiful, sun-kissed afternoon, my yellow Lab Libby and I went for a walk. We passed a mother, her two school-aged kids, and their Lab walking on the trail behind our house. My first thought was, *I wonder why those kids aren't in school?* I quickly dismissed it, figuring that maybe the kids were home-schooled.

As they drew closer, any thoughts I previously had were immediately replaced by the look of sadness on all three faces. Along with the sadness, however, there was also an undertone of lightness I could detect. It was intriguing. Somber, all of them, yet with a slight hint...of what? It appeared to be the slightest hint of peace.

I can't say I noticed much more than that. Their expressions were all I was able to take in at the time; they were so complex. Oh, and there was this low rumbling noise I barely registered. What was that?

As Libby and I got to the end of our path, we turned around and headed back toward home. A few minutes later, I could see the family approaching; they had doubled back, too.

I focused my attention on the dog this time. She was an old girl. I could tell by the way she walked, labored and uneasy, rocking side to side. Although her gait was slow, she was panting hard, forming a perfect "smile" on her sweet Lab face. As I passed the family this second time, I said to the mother, "Now, *that* just makes you want to smile right back," as I nodded to her gentle, old girl.

The mother paused, looked at me with tears in her eyes, and whispered, "Thank you." A moment later and a bit louder, she said, "It's her last day."

The *thank you* came out as more of an exhale, as if she just realized she had been holding her breath.

Within the mother's pauses, I believe she was taking a moment to find her voice. Her strength.

Here was a family demonstrating the art of letting go. As the foursome walked by, I noticed something that had grazed the edge of my mind before. The low rumbling noise I had heard earlier was coming from a red wagon that the daughter was pulling. It was empty inside, except for a yellow, turquoise, and ivory-colored quilt. The family was prepared to carry their girl home if the need arose.

Months later, my thoughts still occasionally drift to this family. The children were not home-schooled; instead, they were given permission to miss a day of school to spend it with a family member who was soon to depart. It was their way of letting go, by taking their girl on a much-loved activity: walking with her beloved family. They were honoring this beautiful Lab, and at the same time, creating a lasting memory of what's important in life.

What *is* important in life? What's important in your life?

Loving. Trusting. Remembering that every day is a blessing. That every living being is a blessing. These are important to me.

Watching this family practice what was important to them, although I was only able to get a glimpse of it, was deeply moving. It served as a reminder to place my focus on Honoring Life and the beautiful act of letting go.

~~~~

"True love doesn't have a happy ending, because true love never ends. Letting go is one way of saying I love you." ~ Anon
~~~~

Fascinated With Stones

"Let me not think of my work only as a stepping stone to something else, and if it is, let me become fascinated by the shape of the stone."
~ Ze Frank

~~~~

As we discussed in "The Window Beyond," an important first step in learning to let go is admitting the truth of a situation. The truth that he let go of you a long time ago. Or the truth that your beloved family member will soon depart. Along with admitting the truth of a situation comes recognizing where your attention lies. Are you focused on the present moment? Or are you focused on the end result? If you are focused on the latter, you've made your job of letting go significantly harder.

I admit I am often focused on the destination; rarely do I enjoy the beauty of the journey. And what a shame. By constantly having my focus on the destination, I not only miss out on opportunities to relish in the now, but I also become attached to the outcome and consequently become disappointed if the outcome is different than what I anticipated. And there's the GOTCHA! *How in the world does that make it*
~~~~

easier to let go? I've been dreaming about the destination (the outcome), putting all of my focus and energy there, and now I've become emotionally invested in *that* outcome, the one I want. I have forgotten a Truth. I have lost sight of trusting in something higher—the Divine holds the full picture view, not I. Unfortunately, I became married to my narrow-view outcome, and now that it has turned out differently, I'm disappointed, maybe even angry, making my tendency to dig in my heels more animated. With heels dug firmly in the ground, roots begin to grow from the soles of my feet and spread down into the earth. Letting go feels impossible when your anchor runs that deep.

Let's stop before we spiral down any further. Instead, let's imagine the stepping stones Ze Frank mentions in the quote above. What about these stepping stones? The bits and pieces along the way helping to take us from point A to point B and from B to C. Picture these stones emerging out of a brook of cool, clear water. Look down and watch the fish, darting this way and that. Each stone is large and sturdy enough to hold your full weight. As you land on each one, crouch down low and run your palm against its smooth surface. Feel its subtle strength beneath you. Become fascinated by its shape.

These stepping stones have been brilliantly

placed on your path. Some are so close together they almost appear as one. Others are placed some distance apart, causing you to steady yourself before you hurl your body forward, only to land securely on the next. Without each stone shaping your journey in its own unique way, no progress would be made along your life-route. You would never reach the beautiful end-goal that awaits you.

Do not rush. Steady yourself. Believe your stone will support you. As you bend down to lower yourself upon your stone's cool, welcoming surface, do not become concerned with the creaking in your bones, the popping of your knees. Instead, see the beauty in the stone's ridges, the life within its curves. Become fascinated by its shape, as you discover the stone *is* your life-route.

Take a moment and drink that in.

Ultimately, trust you are where you are supposed to be. With the trust and deliberate effort to love each stone along your path, you will awake to the feeling of freedom that whispers, *There is nothing to let go of.*

~~~~

"I don't let go of my thoughts—
I meet them with understanding,
then they let go of me."
~ Byron Katie
~~~~

Trust *What* Exactly?

"Woe to the man whose heart has not learned while young to hope, to love— and to put its trust in life."
~ Joseph Conrad

~~~~

This is a story based in Taoism tradition. It is called "The Farmer's Luck."

> There once was a farmer. For many years he tended his crops. One day, his horse managed to break loose and run away. As soon as his neighbors heard the news, they came to visit.
>
> "Such bad luck," they said, eyes downcast, shaking their heads.
>
> "Maybe," the farmer replied.
>
> The next morning when the farmer awoke, he saw that his horse had returned. The farmer also saw two unfamiliar horses with him. His horse had brought two wild horses home.
>
> "Such good luck!" the neighbors cheered.
>
> "Maybe," said the farmer.
>
> The following day, the farmer's son attempted to ride one of the wild horses. He
~~~~

was thrown off and broke his leg. Once again, the neighbors came to offer their sympathy on his misfortune.

"Such bad luck," they said.

"Maybe," offered the farmer.

In the days that followed, a war was announced. Military officials came to the farmer's village to draft young men into the army to fight for their country. Immediately seeing that the farmer's son's leg was broken, they left and went to the next house.

"Such good luck!" exclaimed the neighbors.

"Maybe," replied the farmer.

Ditch the Why and How

Okay, you get it, you see what's happening here. In "The Farmer's Luck," a Truth is illustrated, something we *know* without the need for clarification or explanation. To put into words, the Truth is this:

There are no accidents. Everything happens for a reason.

This Truth has been a driving force in my life; however, I'm sometimes hesitant to say it out loud...and for the silliest reason: because it sounds so cliché. I told you, very silly. But it's true. Everything happens for a reason is a phrase that's thrown around so much, it has lost all of its umph! When you hear it said, you either roll your eyes because you don't believe it or you simply ignore it because of the way it's tossed around so freely. There is no feeling or emotion attached to it. In an effort to get folks to pay attention to it, I like to add another part to the phrase, something that makes it more complete:

Everything happens for a reason, and that reason need not be known.

In order to let go and trust life, I believe you must embrace this whole Truth. In order to let go and fully trust, you must let go of the need to know why something has happened (letting go of the past) or how it will happen (letting go of the future).

In any given situation, we see what we consider to be facts. From these so-called facts, we absorb the context and meaning. It is only now that we form our perception (which may or may not be the truth). Many of us use different techniques and go through various mental exercises to arrive at our conclusions. That's all fine and good, but where we often get tripped up is in trying to understand why a certain thing has happened or how it's going to be resolved. Along with that, we often become so wrapped up in the how, that we become married to the outcome we've envisioned, just like I discussed previously in, "Fascinated With Stones." We become emotionally invested in the outcome of our desire, dreaming about it, praying endlessly, sometimes until the prayer appears more like begging.

Let Go and Trust *What* Exactly?

This is where the practice of letting go and trusting comes in. Let go and trust *what* exactly?

1. Let go of the belief that you must know why something has happened. Instead, trust it happened for your higher good and for the higher good of those around you.
2. Let go of the belief that you must know how it's going to be resolved. Instead, trust it will be resolved for your higher good and for the higher good of those around you.
3. Let go of your attachment to a desired outcome. Instead, trust the outcome will be for your higher good and for the higher good of those around you.

Even if the higher good is not apparent to you, trust.

I say this with much confidence: Once you learn to trust, the events of your life will unfold in miraculous ways, often far better than anything you could have planned or deemed for yourself.

So, just for today, give it a try. Trust. Let go of the need to know why (he broke up with you). Let go of the need to know how (the swooshed-away art ribbons will be returned to you). Try it on, see how it feels. I'm guessing for some it will feel foreign. But I also suspect that with practice it will come to you more easily. As it does, I ask you to pay close attention to the underlying feeling inside you. Is it one of love or one of fear?

Once you're able to feel these love-driven acts of letting go, your inner peace begins to grow. What better motivator to continue practicing trust each day?

I want more peace in my life. So, for today, I choose to let go.

Losing, Letting Go, and Flying Free

Earlier this year, I wrote a series of blog posts on addiction and "losing," although I hadn't set out to write a series on anything. After I had finished writing and posting all six articles that made up the series, I sat back and examined each one more closely–that's when it dawned on me, I had just written the ultimate guide to letting go. The word losing could have been swapped with letting go and the context wouldn't have changed one bit.

One of the posts was called, "7 Things to Lose If You Want to Win." *Win what?* You! The real you that will emerge in a way you'll feel compelled to shout out loud: I Am Free!—that's how one of the articles started out. With each of the items I proposed the reader and I practice "losing," I was actually suggesting we let go of something—something *core* to our being.

Here is a summary of the seven things I suggested we lose (let go of) in order to win ourselves:

1. Lose the disciplined approach – live as you feel.
2. Lose the role you normally play – try something outside of your norm.

3. Lose the mask you don each morning – express your innermost feelings.
4. Lose the notion that you're in control – offer your will to flow with a current larger than you.
5. Lose your adult-like tendencies – see the world and others with child-like eyes.
6. Lose caring what others think of you – don't take anything personally.
7. Lose the constant questions – feel what you feel and act upon that.

Dynamic Duo

Once losing the seven, I suggested we would regain our power. How did I fare, you ask? Well, at first, despite feeling naked in the most vulnerable sense of adult-nakedness (not cute, chubby toddler-nakedness), I ended up being surprised by the Dynamic Duo that showed up: *Confidence and Strength,* which felt quite powerful.

I went on to share the following observations of how it felt to lose me, and asked my readers if they had noticed any of the same feelings/gains during their practice of losing themselves:

1. By losing the disciplined approach, I gained:
    - the courage to be innovative and take risks
    - creative inspiration I didn't know (believe) I had
    - the return of my old "out of the box" thinking
2. By losing the role I normally play, I gained:
    - an awareness of limitless possibilities
    - the needed push to stop hiding
    - firsthand knowledge of what is meant by, "I've taught people how to treat me."
3. By losing the mask I don each morning, I gained:
    - an intimacy with self that wasn't present before I allowed myself to be vulnerable
    - practice at showing up as the genuine me, which gave me confidence to continue
    - the insight that less is more
4. By losing the false notion that I'm in control, I gained:
    - a daily practice of surrender

- seeing the glass as half-full as my primary default
- the knowledge (belief) that I am safe

5. By losing my adult-like tendencies, I gained:
    - a sense of awe and wonder
    - a curiosity that had been lost
    - a desire to see the good in others first

6. By losing the habit of caring what others think about me, I gained:
    - a non-judgmental view of others
    - silence between my ears; the internal monkey-chatter ceased
    - the wholeness of being

7. By losing the constant questions, I gained:
    - more energy to focus on the now
    - experiencing inner clarity
    - simplicity, the gift of seeing life as uncomplicated

Naked No More

With each item I practiced losing, I grew stronger, freer, and more confident. I felt genuine, comfortable in my own skin, naked or clothed. There was no trying to sell myself, no game to play, I simply showed up as me...buyer beware.

And what about the "buyer?" What are they to think? Well, by practicing No. 6 (losing the habit of caring what others think about me), the answer is clearly: *I don't care.* But, if I had to guess, I imagine when you show up as yourself, and you do so repeatedly, the person on the other end breathes an inward sigh of relief. Any anxiety is released, as they ease into the comfort of knowing that with you, "what-you-see-is-what-you-get." By allowing yourself to be seen in all of your glorious *you-ness,* hopefully those mirror neurons will kick in and the other person will follow suit. Before you know it, you'll be sitting around a table with people who have all lost their masks as well.

Without my disciplined approach, without my mask, without all of it, I felt naked. Until I didn't. I practiced until I no longer felt naked. It doesn't stop here though—*I will continue to practice with each new encounter of each new day.* I haven't mastered losing/letting go completely. *Why not?* Because I am human, so I will forget. I am human, so I will allow life to distract me. I am human, so I will give in to fear.

With each practice of exposing more of myself, I honor that which created me and made me enough, just the way I am.

All Together Now

Say (or shout!) out loud with me:

I choose to live wholeheartedly. Today.
I choose to let go. Today.
I choose to believe. Today.
I choose to trust. Today.
I choose peace. Today.
I Am Free. Period.

~~~~

A Step Past Letting Go

All this talking, writing, thinking about letting go, got me questioning one last thing on this topic. When it comes right down to it, if you're actively trying to let go of something, didn't that something happen in the past? And if that something happened in the past, then isn't the current situation not really an issue of letting go at all, but more a matter of accepting *What IS?*

Aye yai yai! I think we just came full circle, friends! Just a little food for thought....
~~~~

8

Pixie Dust

"Above all, watch with glittering eyes the whole world around you, because the greatest secrets are always hidden in the most unlikely places. Those who don't believe in magic will never find it."

~ Roald Dahl

Magical Thinking

To be a child again, unencumbered by not yet "knowing too much," innocent, free. Magical, really. As children, we all had within us not only the capacity but also the desire to use our magical thinking. Playing pretend, imaginary friends, fantasy of all kinds was what our world was about. Interestingly enough, this magical thinking hits its peak and becomes highly developed at approximately four years old, the same age well-meaning parents start to teach us about trust.

Yes, around age four, a child begins to hear and comprehend the message, "Don't talk to strangers. Don't trust that sort of person...." (as the mother or father points to someone who in some way looks "different" than their immediate family). Moments before hearing those words, the child was very possibly not looking at a stranger, but rather at a knight, a princess, or a lion tamer. Now, however, they have assigned a different label with a different *feeling* to the same person.

No one is to blame the parents. Remember, these are well-meaning parents. Parents who have their children's best interest at heart, who only want to protect and teach. Truth be told, hard as I've tried, I imagine I've said numerous things over the years that will play out their own special breed-of-misconception in my boys' lives. But we do our best as parents. So, if your parents taught you that certain people were not to be trusted, think of it this way, your parents were doing the best they knew how; in fact, they may have even had a point in some instances, but as children, we unconsciously tucked away blanket-statements in our minds, not having the intellectual ability to distinguish between the vast number of situations and people we observed. The underlying message we were left with was: *trust is something external to you, something you have no control over*—that is the message that stuck. And that's the part that is untrue.

The Science in Pixie Dust

What *is* pixie dust? First, what's a pixie? Quite simply, a pixie is a fairy. Think Tinker Bell from *Peter Pan*. Tinker Bell enabled humans to fly by sprinkling pixie dust on them as they focused on happy thoughts.

As they believed.

Pixie dust is what you believe. It is your magic. Your very real magic.

So, what is the science behind belief (our pixie dust)? Well, there are numerous studies and books on the topic, my favorite book being *The Biology of Belief*, by Bruce H. Lipton, Ph.D. Without going overboard, let me share a bit about how beliefs are formed and why they are stronger than both feelings and thoughts.

Let's start with a common phenomenon you've likely heard of. It's an expression in neuroscience derived from Donald Hebb, often called Hebb's Rule or Hebbian Theory. It says, "Cells that fire together, wire together." (Sometimes seen as, "*Neurons* or *synapses* that fire together, wire together.") This refers to how neurons adapt during the learning process. Hebb's Rule is not just a saying, it is literally what happens; the more you practice a skill, the better you become, due to your cells (at the synaptic level) continuing to fire together.

What does this have to do with how our beliefs are formed? In short, everything! How we develop our beliefs is the same as how we learn other tasks. Clinical psychologists George Pratt, Ph.D., and Peter Lambrou, Ph.D., describe it this way in their book, *Code to Joy: The Four-Step Solution to Unlocking Your Natural State of Happiness*:

> Through repetition, what started as a response to a singular event becomes progressively strengthened as our synapses grow new neural tissue, laying down an even thicker matrix of nerve fiber. Eventually that response pattern becomes a firmly embedded neural net that represents a fixed way of perceiving the world and events around us.
>
> To use a different analogy: picture the way houseplants shift position and turn to grow in the direction of the sun. In the same way, our synaptic networks shift and grow in the direction of our most emotionally charged thoughts and experiences. This is how we form beliefs: we literally *grow* them, like a dynamic topiary of the mind.
>
> The resulting beliefs are stronger than feelings, deeper than thoughts. Beliefs are patterns of thought so ingrained in our neural networks they have become

> automatic, like entrenched habits of thinking. They are the bedrock of our psychological architecture.

You do realize how spectacular this is, don't you? This means that you have within you the power, the control, the *magic* to create your own pixie dust—*to create your own beliefs.*

But here's the sticky part about beliefs: because our beliefs live in our subconscious brains for the most part, they operate similar to the way we breathe. We are able to regulate/ manipulate our breathing when we think about it, but only when we put our attention there; the majority of the time, we don't give breathing any thought, we simply inhale and exhale. Beliefs work the same way. Unless we are making an effort to think about our beliefs, consciously choosing what we believe, they simply run on auto-pilot.

Remember, you are powerful, powerful, powerful. And so is what you believe.

Hidden Feelings

As you already know, I Love, with a capital "L," reading out loud to my boys. I'm a book junkie and hopefully, by my constant barrage of various literature, my boys will grow up to not only have an appreciation for books, but also have a genuine love for them, too.

When they were younger, before we advanced into more of the pre-teen and Young Adult literature, there was one children's author in particular we sought out and read each and every one of her books. That author was Kate DiCamillo. As a matter of fact, my number one most beloved children's book *ever* was written by her: *The Miraculous Journey of Edward Tulane.* You probably know DiCamillo's work though, from her books that have been made into movies: *The Tale of Despereaux* and *Because of Winn-Dixie.*

What an Odd Place to Hide Your Feelings

When it comes to exploring the concept of *hidden feelings,* DiCamillo's somewhat dark, but thought-provoking children's novel, *The Tiger Rising,* steals the show. As you read a brief summary and excerpt from the onset of the book, allow yourself to consider how you contend with your feelings. Do you have anything in common with Rob Horton, the novel's main character?

Meet Rob Horton

Chapter One starts off very quickly. We immediately get a sense of our main character, a boy named Rob Horton. Within the first three pages of the book we know that Rob spotted an angry tiger pacing in a cage in the woods behind the motel he and his father recently moved into after the death of Rob's mother. We soon discover our protagonist is good at fighting back tears, although he has much to cry about. He misses his mother terribly, he is constantly being bullied at his new school, and he has a horrible, nasty rash on his legs that makes it difficult to get through the day—especially in the damp Florida heat. But Rob is determined *not* to cry. Rob is very good at hiding his emotions, *even from himself.*

From *The Tiger Rising,* DiCamillo writes:

> Rob had a way of not-thinking about things. He imagined himself as a suitcase that was too full, like the one that he had packed when they left Jacksonville after [his mother's] the funeral. He made all his feelings go inside the suitcase; he stuffed them in tight and then sat on the suitcase

> and locked it shut. That was the way he not-thought about things. Sometimes it was hard to keep the suitcase shut. But now he had something to put on top of it. The tiger.
>
> ...and as the first drops of rain fell from the sullen sky, Rob imagined the tiger on top of his suitcase, blinking his golden eyes, sitting proud and strong, unaffected by all the not-thoughts inside straining to come out.

~~~~

What a powerful image DiCamillo paints. I remember thinking, Maybe I should have read this before reading it aloud to the boys—this seems pretty dark. And deep. The metaphors are piling up sky high, and we're only on page four!

What Happens When You Hide Your Feelings?

I decided to continue reading the book out loud. And I'm glad I did! I had underestimated my boys. Even at ages six and nine (at the time), they were ready for the conversations which followed as we became more engrossed in the plot. Today, five years later, I still recall some of the conversations we shared—meaningful discussions around feelings, things like:

- How do you express your feelings?
~~~~

- Where do you express them?
- Is it okay to ever put your feelings in a suitcase?
- What does that even mean?
- What might happen if you were to stuff your feelings in a suitcase?

In response to the last question, I remember very clearly my younger son saying, "Maybe if Rob didn't keep his feelings in a suitcase, his rash would go away."

Hmm.... (And I thought they were too young for such a weighty book.)

What Do You Believe?

I think about what my son said often: "Maybe if Rob didn't keep his feelings in a suitcase, his rash would go away." I wonder...based on my thoughts, my actions, my reactions, *my beliefs,* based on all of it, (including what I attempt to stuff and hide deep down inside), what am I currently manifesting? What are you currently manifesting? Is where you keep your feelings and how you choose to deal with them inconsequential? How could using your magic, your pixie dust, help in solidifying what you believe?

Asking these sorts of questions is important. Exploring them helps us have a better understanding of *What IS*. As you ask yourself these questions about whether or not you hide your feelings and how you express them, try and let go of any critical thoughts. This is not about judging your answers (which is really just judging yourself). Focus instead on the questions themselves and the internal conversations they lead to. Then make a decision: choose how you'd like to *live* your feelings. Choose carefully what you believe as you sprinkle your dust. Ultimately, trust you know what's best for you.

(And please, allow yourself to cry. Express your feelings. Do not stuff them in a suitcase—it will no doubt burst open at a most inopportune moment, especially with no tiger handy to lend his "sitting" assistance.)

Quieting Guilt

There have been times when I have chosen to suppress my feelings and have tried to hide them from the world. Like Rob Horton, I have attempted to hide them from myself. During those times, my feelings have caught up with me in my dreams. Literally.

My biological father passed away in August of 1998 in my hometown, Killeen, Texas. At the time, I was living in Virginia. I had recently started a new job and was three months pregnant with our first child. Between the job, the distance, and *life*, I didn't make it home to Texas very often to see my dad. After his cancer began to "show," after he had gotten really sick, I hadn't seen him at all. I didn't even call much, although I remember thinking I should. Then, after reaching for the phone, I wouldn't. And I didn't.

My last "conversation" with my father was over the phone, where I sat in my cubicle in my new corporate America job, listening to the rhythmic sound of his breathing machine. For this last phone call, I hadn't even called. My mother, then divorced from my father for nineteen years, had called me at work from my father's bedside. She told me that each of my brothers had said their good-byes. Now it was my turn.

Dazed from what felt like being hit on the side of the head with a metal platter, ears still ringing, I went to open my mouth, but instead of intelligible speech, I heard something between a screech and a moan lunge forward, attempting to force its way between my lips. With equal force, I was determined to stifle it. I began to feel light-headed. I needed to sit, but I was standing, something I tend to do, even to this day, during important phone conversations. My eyes darted around, trying to latch on to something that might bring me back to my center. I saw the time displayed on the digital read-out on my phone. It read 1:34 PM. My eyes continued to scan. I landed on a picture of my Cocker Spaniel, tacked directly to the gray cubical wall with a purple push pin. I stared at the dog, the dog who had been my rock through college, my wedding, and eventually the birth of both of our sons, all of the important events of my life it seemed. Every dog person has "the" dog, and I was staring into the eyes of mine, hoping he would once again ground me through another major life event.

After a few more labored breaths, I spoke. My speech was shaky, barely audible, equal parts shame and sadness layered throughout. Truth be told, I'd be generous if I told you I had done a poor job—my good-bye sucked. Although my dad didn't say a word, I'm positive he knew it was me, his Dumpling, on the other end of the line.

Facing Guilt-Ridden Dreams

For years after my father's death, I dreamed about him. There was an eerie sameness in these dreams that was much stronger than in other dreams. The feeling of *realness* in my dad-dreams was incredible. So real, that every time I woke from one, I relived a piece of mourning, at first convinced that he was still alive. I would start by reaching for the phone, ready to dial his number, heavy with feelings of guilt that it had been so long since I had called or visited. But I never actually dialed his phone number. Right before removing the phone from its cradle, the realization would sink in—he was no longer here on this earth. I could not call him. I'd grieve a bit each time I received that dull blow to the gut.

Along with momentarily believing my dad was still alive, I would feel enormous guilt. The feelings of guilt would start long before I'd wake up. There would come a point in each dream where I'd begin to feel ashamed—ashamed that I had somehow abandoned him. And I would wonder, *Will he forgive me? Will he welcome me, although I very seldom call or visit? What kind of person does this...especially when her father is clearly so ill?*

Another constant in my dad-dreams was that at some point, I actually would make that phone call or interrupt life long enough to take that trip back to Texas to see him, only to find that he had been cured! What a glorious moment in the dream! The cancer had inexplicably left his body and he was back to being completely healthy! Somehow, I had missed the beauty of his recovery and I would find myself feeling initially forlorn that I hadn't been there to witness it, but climactically ecstatic for his recovery. While still asleep, I would silently vow to become the dutiful daughter that I had not been. I would call and visit him all the time. I had been given a second chance to make things right now that he was healed! But before those thoughts had completely gelled in my far-off, dreaming mind, I knew they were lies. I knew I was lying to myself. At best, I'd call him immediately (which I would again try to do as soon as I awoke), but I already knew I wouldn't keep it up long-term. And the flood of guilt and sadness would wash over me anew.

What Haunts You, Hunts You

All during the dreams, while still asleep, I felt guilt and sadness at every turn. Guilt that I hadn't called. Sadness that I missed witnessing and celebrating his remarkable dream-recovery. Guilt that I knew as good as my intentions were, I would once again become the lame daughter and say that "life" had gotten in the way. Sadness when I woke up and realized he was not alive. Guilt that I hadn't prayed more. Sadness because I missed him.

Guilt. Sadness. Guilt. Sadness. Oscillating back and forth like a fan stuck in the *On* position, without an *Off* switch or a plug to yank out of the damn wall.

This clearly felt like a haunting. And the nature of how the same elements and themes of the dream repeated themselves, time and time again, *that* felt like a hunting.

Quieting the Guilt-Ridden State

Those dreams have not visited me in quite some time. What might surprise you is even with all the sadness and guilt I felt with each dad-dream, I would earnestly welcome them if they ever returned. Each time they presented themselves, their bitter-sweetness became a shawl, draping my shoulders and edging out the chill. The fact is, I'd gladly take all of the guilt and sadness to have the brief feeling, the *belief,* that my father was still alive. During those dreams, I could feel his radiant presence. If only for a few moments, I could feel him—a man who led a life filled with equal parts goodness and perniciousness. In my dream state, I only felt the goodness. Maybe because all I ever wanted, was to see the goodness in him. And it would melt my still-sleeping heart every time.

Do you know what that tells me about our ability to actually *feel* what we *believe?* To create what we believe?

What we believe has *powerful strength.*

No doubt, what we believe does have powerful strength. Here I sit, retelling a story from my life, that before writing about it, I had never told a soul. In admitting that I would choose to relive the guilt, the sadness, the shameful feelings of being an absent daughter, even a small bit of the mourning process, I have given myself the *gift of release.* I no longer suppress the guilt and sadness, I no longer stuff them down or try to hide them. No, along with the gift of release, I no longer keep the guilt and sadness trapped in my body. And with that, I have been able to live a true example of how powerful our beliefs are—so powerful I believed a dead man alive. If only for a moment, *I believed.*

What guilt-ridden dreams are you living? How are you choosing to face them? My hope for you is that you are choosing a way that serves you well. That you're able to move through whatever guilt and sadness exist and apply what you've learned—to live the most fulfilling life possible.

This is a heavy story. True. And I realize I don't give you the answer to how you should go about facing your guilt-ridden dreams. I don't need to. I believe that your answer lies firmly within and between the lines above, as well as within you. Trust yourself to hear the answer within your pixie dust. Begin by trusting yourself.

From Pixie Dust to Sweeping Dust (and back again)

As adults, we allow our magic to fade; we allow life to become very serious. We choose to sweep dust, say, when a parent dies. We choose to sweep dust when our heart breaks. Sweeping, tidying, cleaning, pushing our magic down.

But there is magic to be found in adulthood. It is here, in adulthood, where we address the unfinished work of childhood. It is here we are able to feel and appreciate our inner peace—a time when we have the tools to address and heal any early wounds that may still linger. We now understand the magic that lies within each of us: We are magnificent beings. We determine our beliefs. We no longer rely on a false sense of control over a situation, but rather understand that we are only in control of our preparation for what *might* happen and how we respond to what *has* happened. Ultimately, we choose to see our magic. We sprinkle our pixie dust. We believe, let go, and trust.

~~~~

> "Tell me one last thing," Harry asked of Dumbledore. "Is this real? Or has this been happening inside my head?"
~~~~

Dumbledore beamed at him, and his voice sounded loud and strong in Harry's ears even though the bright mist was descending again, obscuring his figure.

"Of course it is happening inside your head, Harry, but why on earth should that mean that it is not real?"

~~~~

"What you believe has more power than what you dream or wish or hope for. You become what you believe."
~ Oprah Winfrey
~~~~

9

Quite Simply, Peace

"Our desire for peace must be stronger than our attachment to our misery, our ego, or our need to be right."
~ Jill Bolte Taylor

Peace, Love, and Happiness

At the beginning of this book I shared with you my belief that we, as humans, seek peace more than any other single thing in this world. Yes, *even more than love or happiness*. I told you there would be more on this topic later. Well, it's later.

The truth about love is that it is complicated. Love is beautiful, but it can be messy. To truly love another involves becoming vulnerable, something many of us find difficult to do. I can love someone and at the same time allow myself to feel hurt by their actions. When this happens, I feel anything but peace. I must work through the hurt in order to get to the other side, and only then do I regain my peace. Peace, on the other hand, is not complicated. It's not messy. It lies beneath love as a soft, welcoming cushion. Peace is fundamental to love.

Loving unconditionally is Love's Truth. To love unconditionally is something we do as infants and small children, until...we don't. Not until I had children of my own did I truly feel (remember) what it feels like to love another unconditionally. Unconditional love is something I'm currently studying. In theory, there is no reason why I cannot love each person I meet unconditionally, but in truth, it's still part of my daily practice—I'm not there yet.

As for happiness? Without peace, it's impossible to find happiness. When asked the question, "What do you want more than anything else in the world?" isn't the common answer, "To be happy"? Followed by a close runner-up, "To feel love." Love and happiness—we all want them. Without peace, both become challenging to experience.

Underneath the feelings of love and happiness lies something that feels more concrete, yet simultaneously gives the feeling of being light, airy, and all-engulfing. That feeling is peace. *Peace is solid, firm, and more of a foundation than anything else I've ever experienced.* In that sense, it's more real than love and happiness in satisfying our inner needs, wants, and desires. Peace is the feeling you experience when you are in step with your own, unique rhythm.

This is why I believe we seek peace more than anything else, whether we know it or not.

Today I Feel Peace Like That

Your desire to live in harmony with your true essence is great—you know it when you feel it. And whether you agree with me or not on the hierarchy/position of peace, love, and happiness, I feel confident you will agree that it's difficult to feel any one of these if you're gripped with fear and worry.

Join me as I share with you the following story of a morning that would have normally been fear-filled or at least anxiety-filled, but instead, was peace-filled.

This is the story I shared on my blog the morning I underwent the last of my surgeries after being diagnosed with breast cancer. It was a re-blog actually. See, when I sat down to write the article for that particular day, I realized I had already written about where I wanted to be that morning (emotionally). Here is what I shared:

"Peace Like That"

We've heard it said that a picture is worth a thousand words. Well, when I took the following picture, I only felt one word: *Peace*

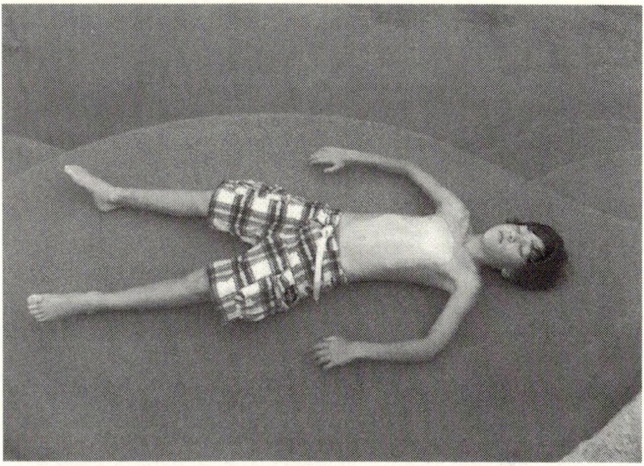

Right before I snapped this photo, my son felt my presence and opened his eyes; he even began to sit up. I was sure I had missed the opportunity to capture such a state of calm; there was no way he could lull himself into such peaceful bliss again. But within seconds, he was back, as serene as you see him now. *I was amazed at how quickly he was able to let go.*

Looking closely, you'll notice that only the tips of his toes, his stomach and chest, and a portion of his face are exposed. I suppose the water surrounding his body like that, coupled with the slight hint of air brushing his skin, made for a magical combination. Over the past week I've looked at this picture dozens of times. As I look at it, I try and imagine what it feels like to feel that much peace. I especially focus on his face.

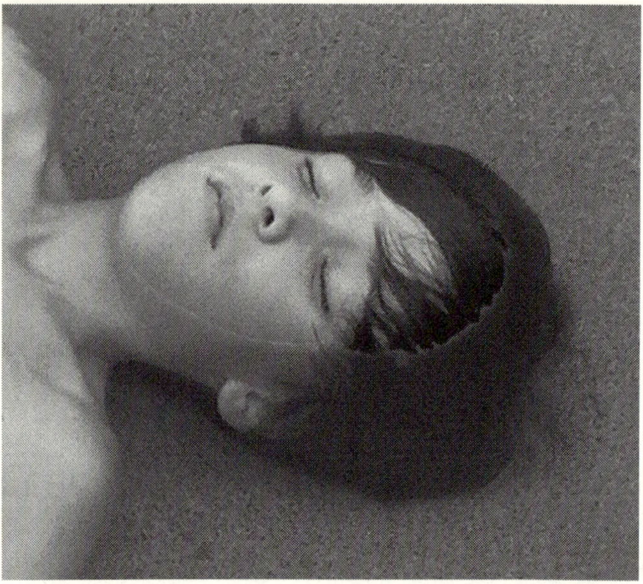

Clearly, he's not worried about anything. His ears are submerged so he's not distracted by any outside noise, but rather he's experiencing that muffled sense of sound like one does when under water. He feels air on his face and trusts his next breath will come. He knows (believes) he has a secure foundation underneath him that will not betray him. Somehow he even knows his brother and friend will not jump in the pool and disturb his peace, or perhaps he doesn't care. *He's not concerned about anything in this moment.*

I want peace like that.

Treading Water

Many times (yesterday, for instance) I rush around so much, I feel as if life is moving too fast. When it's three o'clock in the afternoon and I haven't eaten breakfast or lunch yet, there's a problem. Around that time the phone rang, and although I knew I was feeling terribly depleted and extremely hungry, I chose to pick it up anyway. Moments later I heard myself say out loud that things are so hectic I feel I'm barely keeping my head above water. My girlfriend laughed and said, "Sounds like a good topic for your next post!" Exasperated, I remember thinking, *But I already have a topic—I am going to write about the picture of my son above and the peace within.*

And it hit me! My son and I both had our heads above water, he literally, and I figuratively, but he wasn't feeling the anxiety I was. His way was serving him well—mine was not.

Over time I've studied this picture, trying to capture the essence of the peace he was feeling. I shared the picture with my mom and discussed with her the peace I feel when I look at it. Then, somewhere along the way, I allowed myself to move way too fast. I allowed myself to get caught up with the next, and the next, and the next, instead of *Being*. I was holding on to *doing*, instead of *being*, and as a result I was feeling weighed down.

Moments later, rummaging around in my office, I saw a quote by Buddha: "Life can only take place in the present moment. If we lose the present moment, we lose life."

Lose life? No! *I treasure life*. I *trust life*. How can I honor this life that the Divine has given me by allowing myself to spin out of control with my thoughts and actions? Now, stopping long enough to acknowledge what I had been doing, stopping long enough to become aware, I stopped, period. I began to simply *Be*. I let go and felt free.

~~~~

I'm happy to share with you, that *Today, I Feel Peace Like That*—the same peace you see in the photograph of my son—peace I did *not* feel at the time I originally wrote this post, *but I do now*. So today, as you think of me, of the surgeons and the medical staff attending to me, please find it somewhere inside yourself to also feel *Peace Like That*. To let go and feel free.

And so it is. Amen.
~~~~

An Offering For Your Beloved

What cures insomnia?
Why trust at all?
What do people want in life more than anything else?
What one thing do I wish most for my children?
What one thing do I wish most for anyone I love?

What do all of these questions have in common?

Drumroll please.... Answer: *Inner Peace!* What? Not sexy enough for you? Not exciting enough? Maybe not even exciting enough to warrant an "!" Or earth-shattering enough to wake you in the middle of the night in a cold sweat, screaming, *"I need more peace in my life!"* No. That's not how peace rolls. Peace is one of those things that falls in the "out-of-sight, out-of-mind" category, similar to the foundation of your house. But without it—well, your house won't last very long as the strong, stable structure you've grown to rely on to support your outer needs. Peace, my friends, is what supports your innermost needs. And for that reason, I find it sexy and exciting as all get-out, regardless of its knack for subtlety.

Here's What I Know about Inner Peace:

- Peace is a *present-moment-thing*; it occurs in the here and now.
- Therefore, don't go chasing after peace; it isn't a good idea since it's not a future event.
- Similarly, you may have had peace in your past, but if you don't feel it now, in your present, there's no use longing or lamenting—you're just wasting your time.
- When you feel peace in your present, acknowledge it, honor it—find ways to celebrate it.
- The more you trust yourself, the more you will experience peace.
- My belief that the Divine lives within each of us allows me to trust with all of my heart and mind—bringing more inner peace in my life. This can work for you, too.
- Peace and inner conflict cannot exist simultaneously.
- Once I learned how trust works, peace entered my life, and the insomnia I battled off and on for nearly twenty years simply stopped.
- Peace does not necessarily mean quiet.

Peace Can Look Different For Each of Us

So, what exactly does peace look like? Feel like? I'm sure you've felt it before. But to describe it, I'd say for me:

- Looking deeply into my eyes in the mirror and seeing someone who has learned to appreciate her outer beauty as well as her inner beauty feels like peace.
- Sipping my cuppa tea with a still mind, I feel peace.
- Being gentle with myself. I would never invite someone back into my life who spoke to me as harshly as I sometimes speak to myself. When I get it right and am gentle with myself, I feel peace.
- Observing the rise and fall of my boys' torsos as they sleep, and then realizing I've unconsciously been matching their breathing, feels like peace.
- The expression on my yellow Lab's face 99.9 percent of the time looks like peace.

Ultimately, inner peace feels like a calming in your heart.

That's what I know (believe) about peace. That's how peace looks and feels to me. Desirous, grounding, alive, freeing, and, yes, even sexy and exciting, all at the same time. How about you? What do you know (believe) about peace? How does it look and feel in your life? If you're running low on examples and you very seldom feel peace in your life, start small: maybe sit still and watch the rise and fall of your abdomen, and do nothing else, think nothing else. Simply observe the rise and fall for one full minute. You, *yes you*, as busy as you are, have sixty seconds.

Love yourself enough to support your innermost needs by offering Your Beloved *(you!)* sixty seconds of inner peace right now.

A Woman At Peace With Her Body

Find a woman at peace with her body and after you get over the shock, stop and take in the serene look on her face. That would be the look of peace.

A few weeks after my final surgery, I was home enjoying a mid-afternoon snack of cheese and crackers at our kitchen table when my mother called to check on me. I remember mentioning to her that I was feeling great, except for being a little annoyed. "Oh, yeah? What's going on?" she asked. "It's all these cracker crumbs I keep finding all over my chest!"

"Your chest? What do you mean? Where did they go before?"

"My lap!" I told her.

See, I have a much different body now than I did *before*. A body that collects crumbs, as if they were landing on a shelf, instead of making a direct descent to my lap! Boy, did we laugh at that one! But it's true. My body has changed. And along with the physical changes came the emotional changes. Those, I must admit, have not been as humorous. They've been quite eye-opening—freeing is more accurate, as if I've somehow grown more into me.

Detached Woman

Going through reconstructive surgery was one of those things that, had I not gone through it, I never would have guessed I would feel the way I did. About my body. About being a woman. About my femininity in general.

After being told the cancer was gone, to say I breathed a sigh of relief would be an understatement. Cancer gone? *Par-taay!* Woot, woot, with both hands in the air, and some sassy hip action to match! So when the doctors began talking to me about the rebuild, I remember saying something like, "Whatever. I'm sure they'll look fine. Do what you need to do."

I was pretty detached. They're just breasts, right? They served their purpose when I nursed my babies, didn't they? What more was there?

I'm guessing at this point I should explain that I see the world in terms of function first. Later *maybe*, if someone points it out to me, I may notice a more subtle nuance, such as beauty. For me, I hadn't considered my body in terms of beauty, or shape, or any distinctly feminine quality. You have this body, you see yourself day after day (without really seeing yourself at all), and over time your body morphs and changes into its current state—that's just the way it works. It's no wonder a thing like beauty could evade you. Or at least, evade me.

However, as the reconstruction process began and I watched my body change, week by week enduring the discomforting (borderline painful) expansion process, my attitude also changed. Was an inner woman emerging?

Size Does Matter

As if cancer-free weren't bonus enough, *I now had a say in size!* I could finally have my upper body match my lower body!

I remember in the second grade, I was at my friend Shannon's house for a swimming party. I was running around in a Pepto-Bismol-pink bikini with white polka dots. It was a ridiculous looking thing, the shade of pink was all wrong, the polka dots didn't help, and it had two rows of these frilly ruffles on both top and bottom. (Must have been on sale, because I had one in turquoise, too.) I had hopped out of the pool to make a mad dash to the bathroom, and as I returned, I stopped a few steps short of the patio, positioning myself behind a large leather recliner. My mother's friends were talking about me, specifically about my "shape." I watched them, as they seemed to be communicating in looks and gestures more than words. The words they did manage to utter were in hushed tones, too quiet for me to make out. But it was in their eyes. The way they looked at each other knowingly, nodding their heads with a raised brow, as if everyone was in agreement. *Agreement about what?* At the time, I didn't understand this silent form of woman-talk, but I knew it meant something. Something was wrong, and it had something to do with me, with my girl-shape. My mother didn't say a word, and I never mentioned it until I was in my forties. But in the days, months, and years that followed the pink, polka dot bathing suit scene, that second-grade girl just kept looking in the mirror. Wondering. Scrutinizing. Eventually, as I grew older, I understood.

Matching Hips and Breasts

Like I said, now with the help of reconstructive surgery, my upper body would match my lower body. I was determined that my new breasts would match my hips. So, as my plastic surgeon and I discussed the reconstruction, when the topic landed on size, I would tell him the same thing every time: "Even me out, Doc. Once you've balanced my top-half with my bottom-half, then stop."

So that's exactly what he did: he balanced me out.

Here's what the typical process of "balancing out"—or getting a woman to their desired size after mastectomy (if they choose this option)—looks like. After the breast tissue is removed in the initial surgery to eradicate the cancer, these things called tissue expanders are placed where the breasts once were. It's brilliant, really. When the woman wakes up from surgery, she looks down and sees what the surgeon refers to as the "breast mound." By surveying her body (over the hospital-issue bra), and seeing the shape of her body, psychologically she doesn't feel the degree of loss she otherwise would. Essentially, you look the same. You are still the same size, just with some added bandages and a bra to cover the incisions. Throughout the weeks that follow, you visit your plastic surgeon, where he or she will begin a weekly expansion process. The surgeon injects saline into the tissue expanders through a port located on the side of the expander. You repeat this process until you reach the size you want. And *voila*!

Week after week, as I was losing my former shape, I was simultaneously gaining not only a new shape, but also an altered perception of myself. The way I thought of myself was changing. I was beginning to *see* myself for the first time. The little girl, the second-grade girl who grew to be ashamed of her hips, was slowly evaporating into the heavens, and at the not-so-ripe age of forty-one, a woman was emerging. I began to embrace a femininity that I formerly didn't feel entitled to...although I wasn't even aware of it at the time. This was a classic case of "I didn't know what I didn't know."

What Does All This Breast Talk Mean?

On one hand, I still think, "They're just breasts, right?" I mean, I didn't go so overboard that they enter the room before I do. They don't define me or change who I am on the inside.

Wrong. Although my breasts don't define me, and they haven't changed who I am at my core, the way I *see* myself has changed. I'm much more loving of my physical body. I embrace my body in a way I never did before. Scars, fading bruises, extra weight I'm carrying—none of that gets me too excited or worked up anymore. I recognize my body has been through a lot, and I'm gentle in my thoughts toward it. I believe this is a part of the healing process that goes deeper than scars, bruises, or temporary weight gain.

Gentle. Loving. Embracing. Healing. I see the beauty in the feminine. I see the beauty in me. And if that isn't the feeling of peace—a woman loving her body—then I don't know what is.

It simply feels freeing. *I am free.*

Continue On Your Path, Move Forward, Journey

Fast forward one year for a Celebration-of-Self! For the one-year anniversary of being cancer-free, I celebrated my good health with a close girlfriend at a spa in Sedona, Arizona. The spa was named Mii Amo, which in the Native American Yuman language means:

To continue on one's path, moving forward, or journey.

As my friend Brandee and I were getting settled into our room, we noticed scrolls on our beds. Their contents set the tone for the quiet introspection that would follow. As you read the prayer-like words, pay close attention to what speaks to you and see what you can toss in your little red wagon as you continue on your path, move forward, and journey.

Our scrolls read:

> Everything is as it should be and I recognize the perfection in my life daily.
>
> Today, I will do my best and trust that is enough.
>
> I am responsible for my attitude and I look for the good in everything.

I create my reality, and I focus on what is good and right in my life and the world around me.

My positive attitude reflects in the people I come in contact with today.

I release my need to be a victim, realizing I always have a choice.

Opportunities abound for me always.

I release the need to please all of the people all of the time, and recognize it is enough to please myself.

These intentions are to help guide your discoveries and the transformations you may make during your journey.

~~~~

Eight short lines. Eight deep intentions. Eight meaningful prayers.

What a beautiful way to start a journey.

What a beautiful, peaceful way to start each day of your life.

Amen.
~~~~

10

Trust, Period.

"Without trust, words become the hollow sound of a wooden gong. With trust, words become life itself."
~ John Harold

Growing Forward

You've heard people say, "I'm moving forward with my life." Or, "Let's go forward with this project." People run forward. They even stumble forward, sometimes in what appears to be the dark. Move, go, run, stumble, crawl, stagger—there are many ways to expend your energy in a forward direction.

But how about growing forward? Similar to how a flower grows with the proper soil, adequate water, and ample sunlight, we experience human growth. Our human growth takes into account factors such as nutrition, exercise, sleep, and yes, even the love we give and receive.

That's one type of growth, human growth. However, that's not the same growing forward you do when you are on your spiritual path. While on your spiritual path, you grow forward on a soul level. You grow forward in your quest for Truth. You grow forward in your love of self. You grow forward as you learn to trust.

Before I began to study the nature of trusting, I held the belief that to "master" trust, one must learn to trust others. The better you got at trusting others, the more skilled you were at trusting, period. It made perfect sense at the time.

Later, I came to see it very differently. Like most things in life, placing the focus outwardly is not the ticket. Outward focus typically has to do more with ego, lack of confidence, or taking the easy way out. By directing our efforts and attention inward, beginning with trusting and loving ourselves, that's where the shift occurs. The magic. On the inside. That's where true trust begins.

Does that mean you won't ever experience betrayal? That you won't endure hurt? Or that all of your fears and worries will disappear forever? No, no, and no...you may still experience betrayal, hurt, fear, and worry. What it means, is that instead of plotting how to protect yourself, or spending countless hours trying to predict what another person is going to say or do, you stop all of that outward, externally aimed effort and *look inside first.*

As a pretty benign example, let's say you're having a touchy conversation with your neighbor Tom—you can see it either going in this direction or that direction. Your mind starts to wander. You start to worry and begin guessing what Tom's motives are. *Why is he saying that? What does that even mean? Is he deliberately trying to get under my skin? What's his angle?* Rather than trying to figure out why Tom's saying what he is, or trying to figure out what Tom's going to say next (outward focus, your focus is on Tom), instead, lead from a place of knowing, believing that no matter what Tom's actions are, *you can trust yourself enough* to react in such a way that supports your best interest. Let me say that again. *Trust yourself enough to react in your best interest.* It has nothing to do with Tom, with what he says or doesn't say, with what he does or doesn't do. Your attention is on *you.*

Love and Trust, Trust and Love

Once you're able to trust yourself and know (believe) you can handle any situation that comes your way, what other people say or do almost becomes irrelevant. This is where the shift, the magic I spoke of, enters the picture. The magic is this: you now trust-love yourself enough to act in your best interest. *But what does that look like, you ask?* It looks like this—you trust-love yourself enough not to tolerate others' continued hurtful behavior. You trust-love yourself enough to know when to stop and when to continue (a diet, a job, a marriage, a friendship, a "fill in the blank"). You trust-love yourself enough to know (believe) that if the choice you made isn't working out well for you, you're not a failure; it's simply time to make another choice (remember Thomas Edison and his 10,000 light bulb attempts?). You trust-love yourself enough.

Once I understood and embraced this, I experienced a *Grow Forward* moment unlike any I had witnessed before. It was as if I were strapped to a star and the higher we rose and the more brilliantly we shone, the more Truth we embodied. You are your own brilliantly shining star. You too can grow forward, grow more into who you were put on this Earth to be.

Patience, no matter what language you speak, is fundamental when learning anything worthwhile. Learning to trust doesn't happen all at once. And even once you think you've got it down, you're a total Trust Master, and in your eagerness, you reach over to check the box labeled: *Trust Complete*, followed by crossing the word *Trust* off your to-do list—don't. That's not the way it works. Trusting yourself, loving yourself—they are both daily practices. And they both start from within.

~~~~

"You can search throughout the entire universe for someone who is more deserving of your love and affection than you are yourself, and that person is not to be found anywhere. You, yourself, as much as anybody in the entire universe, deserve your love, [trust], and affection."
~ Buddha
~~~~

Truths

It's fair to say that each individual piece I've written for this book has as its main character Trust. Sometimes Love dominated a segment, or often Letting Go or *What IS*, but no matter how obvious or how subtle a story was, this book has trust as its pulse.

I wanted you to get a feel for trust first, through the stories I shared, before offering a definition of trust. I wanted you to feel the potential of trust. How it leads to peace. How letting go is key. How what we believe is our own, personal, very powerful pixie-dust magic. And how all of these elements work together in their own unique flow.

Now that you have a taste for trust and you know what it feels like within the context we've been discussing, let me reiterate a simple definition of trust that appeared in "Swooshed Away, The Faith of a Child": *Trust means to follow the heart.* Trust means to follow *your* heart, trusting what is within you.

I encourage us all to look inward. Look inside ourselves and believe that the amount we trust depends on how strongly we know (believe): I've got this! I can handle this...whatever *this* may be.

And although I've mentioned this before, it's worth stating again—along with understanding this fundamental truth that trust begins from within, comes a bigger truth: *God dwells within you*. You are taken care of. You are not alone in your worries, your struggles, your joys, or your triumphs.

~~~~

"All I have seen teaches me to trust the creator for all I have not seen."
~ Ralph Waldo Emerson
~~~~

Afterword

I've enjoyed sharing stories with you that exemplify trusting oneself. When I first started writing about trust on my blog, I had no clue what was coming down the pike for me. I had no idea to prepare for something as life altering as what I experienced after being diagnosed with breast cancer—not for myself and not for my family. But Life has given me skills. Precious gifts. How absolutely ironic that all my years of studying trust would lead me to write about trust, only to have me live it out publicly on my blog. Hmm...ironic or synchronistic?

Whether it's an illness, a marriage, a divorce, a promotion, the birth of a child, a car accident, a whatever...it doesn't stop there. Life continues with its joys and struggles. And as it unfolds, you will continue to have choices every step of the way. Choices about how you perceive others' words and actions, choices about your reactions to those words, choices about how and when you're ready to let go. Choices about all of it. But I must say, loving yourself, trusting yourself—that's where it all begins. *That's where it's at!*

Who knows what this next year holds for me? For you? Who knows what tomorrow holds for us? Are you ready to have your actions be led by love and not by fear? Are you ready to live your life with trust? Trusting there is a greater, Divine force in existence, even if you don't know how or why or even by what name to call the awesome force many know as God?

So as I say good-bye for now, I leave you with one final hope and a prayer:

My hope is that the questions of *Why me? Why is this happening to me?* have abated for you—that you are no longer led by such questions that raise fears and worries, no longer believe that you must earn trust or that trust can be taken away from you. Rather, I hope that you feel the freedom of living with a deep sense of inner peace, knowing that love and trust begin with you first. Believing. Trusting.

I pray that you lead your life by Love and live your life with Trust. Amen.

"Meet Trust's Cousin"
Kristi & Leslie
Acapulco, Mexico 1993

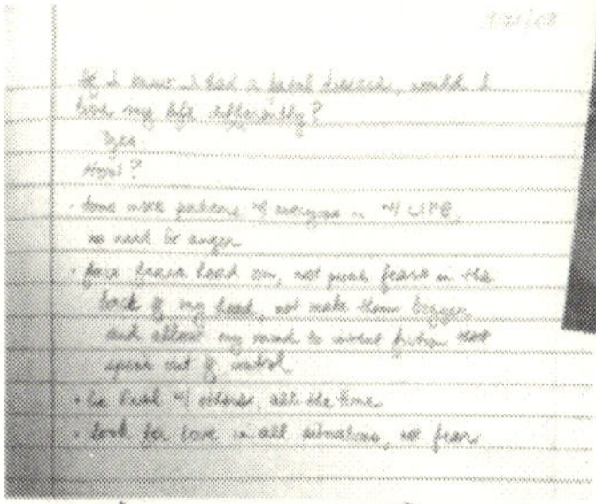

"Knowing When You Are Predicted To Die"

"What Do You Own?"

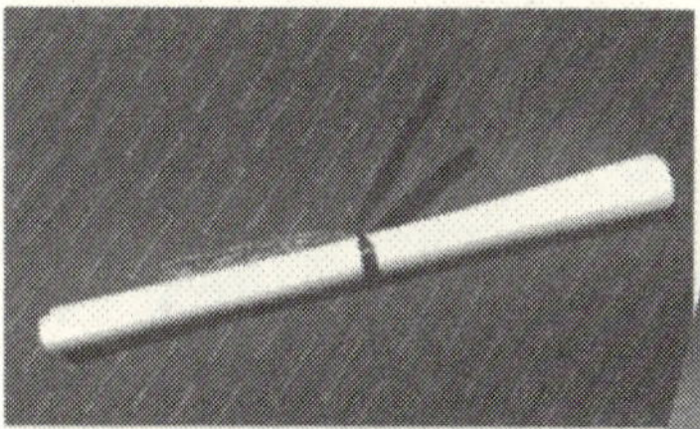

"Continue On Your Path, Move Forward, Journey"

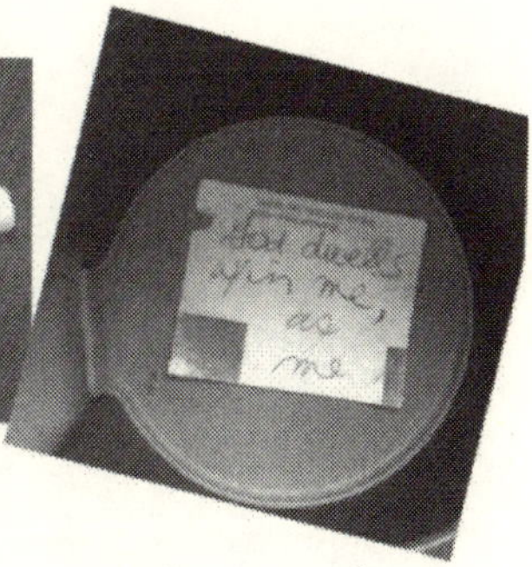

"cword"

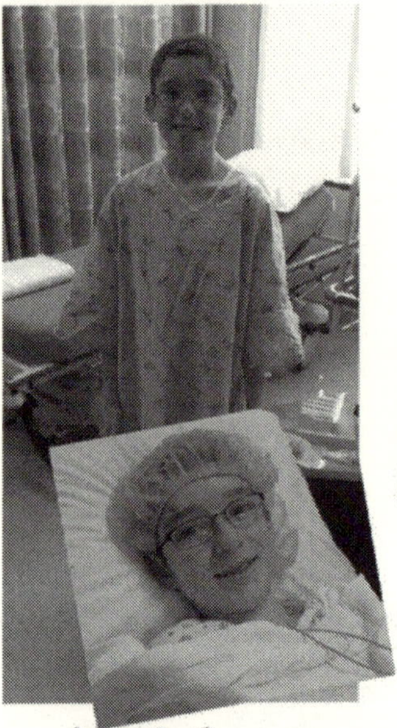

"Goofy-Juice or Confidence?"

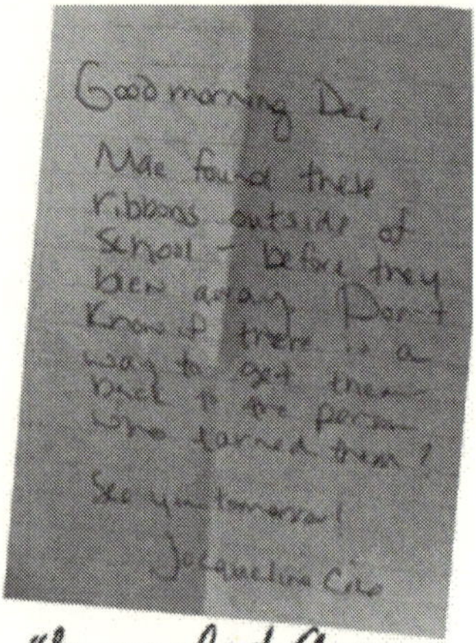

"Swooshed Away, The Faith of a Child"

"The Window Beyond"

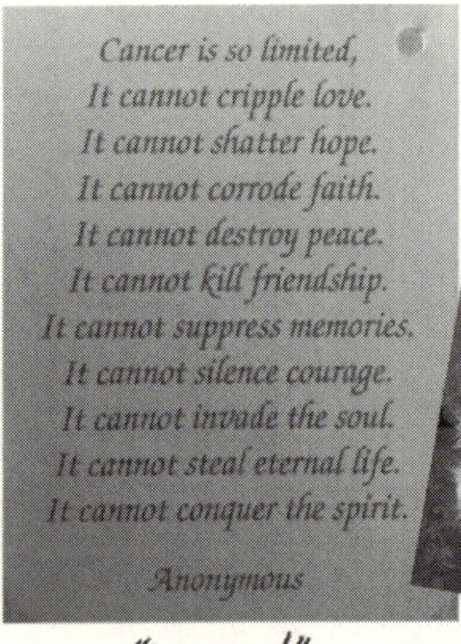

Cancer is so limited,
It cannot cripple love.
It cannot shatter hope.
It cannot corrode faith.
It cannot destroy peace.
It cannot kill friendship.
It cannot suppress memories.
It cannot silence courage.
It cannot invade the soul.
It cannot steal eternal life.
It cannot conquer the spirit.

Anonymous

"C-word"

Faith the Lamb

About The Author

At my center, I am a teacher. Whether a speech pathologist, elementary school teacher, retail manager, corporate America employee, Pilates instructor, writer, daughter, friend, mother—it doesn't matter, I have teaching as my rhythmic pulse.

I began exploring trust in 1998 shortly after my father passed away. Before long I became a student of trust, eventually putting trust to practice and seeing how learning to trust yourself forges a direct path to peace. The more I learned to trust myself, the more freedom I felt. The easier life became.

And then I was diagnosed with breast cancer. Talk about an opportunity to practice trust; it was either that or be consumed with fear and worry. I chose to practice trust.

Today I connect with others through my blog, radio show, and live talks. I light up like a Christmas tree in Rockefeller Center when I hear from a reader or see a spark ignite in someone sitting in the audience—that spark that says, "Yes, this is possible! I can learn to love myself. I can learn to trust myself. I can feel the tug of freedom as peace enters my life, as I learn to let go of fear and worry."

Why is that so important to me?

Because I received a gift years ago when I learned to love and trust myself. Because I am here on this Earth to make a difference by sharing that gift with you.

I am someone who wants to be Seen. And See others. I am someone who is guided by my head, but consciously seeks ongoing heart guidance. I am someone who has learned to trust—not by mastery—but by the daily practice of letting go.

As is the case with any devoted teacher, I am also a student, interested in continuous learning and growth. Books, life experiences, hardships, joys, connecting with others, these are all excellent teachers for the Life Student. Sharing our stories and who we are with one another encourages our ongoing development and learning. *Thank you for contributing to my growth by allowing me to share my stories with you.*

Where to find me

- On my blog: www.TrustLifeToday.com
- Facebook group page: Love, Trust & Pixie Dust
- Weekly radio show: Love, Trust & Pixie Dust (found at PixieDustRadio.com)
- Twitter: @trustlifetoday
- Email: leslie@trustlifetoday.com
- Somewhere quiet, sipping a cuppa tea
- In the Pilates studio
- Walking my yellow Lab

(not necessarily in that order)

I would be honored if you reviewed this book. Thank you.

Made in the USA
Middletown, DE
17 August 2021

46263136R00146